Advance Praise for *A Da...*

"From rhythmic Gaelic blessings … to Earthrise as seen from Apollo 8; from ancient heartfelt yearnings of the soul … to family memories that evoke the eternal—the Rev. Dr. Joanna Seibert collects for us the gems that encircle and fill in our spiritual heritage, in preparation for that yearly season of longing: the Advent, Christmas, and Epiphany cycle. Drawing on literary traditions, artists' works, and reflections from decades of faithfulness, her *Daily Spiritual Rx for Advent, Christmas, and Epiphany* is brimming with insights and challenges, along with warm affirmations and stirring hopes that cradle the Christian life. The vibrant quotes and interpretations that shine through this work will offer hours of deep self-searching as well as whimsical delight, as the reader travels through a much-loved season with new and old friends. As Joanna brightens our in-boxes with her Daily Something, in this book she brings together a richness of personal understanding, braided through the thoughts and wisdom of the saints."

—Isabel Anders is the author of *Becoming Flame, Awaiting the Child,* and other titles.

"As I read the Rev. Dr. Joanna Seibert's new book *A Daily Spiritual Rx: A physician, minister, and spiritual director shares spiritual direction insights for Advent, Christmas, and Epiphany,* the image of a shimmering, multi-faceted star kept popping up in my mind. Seibert barely mentions a star, if at all, but it is an apt image for her guidebook through the triptych of the Nativity Season. *A Daily Spiritual Rx* takes the reader on a tour of the writings of contemporary and ancient Christians who enhance Seibert's Nativity journey. She directs us to spiritual practices and 12-Step wisdom to help us make this journey. As tour guide she uses her multi-faceted experience as physician, minister, grief counselor, and spiritual director to infuse the trip with compelling personal stories prompted by the writings and practices. This book is not an end in itself, but a resource, a guiding light, a bright star for exploring the depth and breadth of Advent, Christmas, and Epiphany."

—Sybil MacBeth is the author of *Praying in Color: Drawing a New Path to God* and *The Season of the Nativity: Confessions and Practices of an Advent, Christmas, and Epiphany Extremist.*

"In her latest book, *A Daily Spiritual Rx for Advent, Christmas, and Epiphany*, a doctor, priest, spiritual mentor, musician, and woman of faith brings her discerning observations to a season so often stripped of its glory and anguish for slick magazine covers and smiling Amazon boxes. Reading Dr. Joanna Seibert's entries through the seasons of waiting and manifestation feels like an open diary into which one can slip, then, in turns, walk, ponder, fall, whisper, doubt, and hope alongside a flesh-and-blood friend. Her words introduce us to and remind us of the piercing, messy story of God's incarnation. Seibert is acutely aware of our tendency to holiday distraction as we search vainly for the tidy, neat and perfect versions of these holy days. Drawing us in to the sweet picture of St. Lucia and a picturesque Christian celebration, we imagine the wreath of little girls, ' … the bonfires with incense and the candlelight parades.' The image, however, is interrupted by the reality of death as the author describes how she lost two friends on this precise feast day, friends who brought light into her darkness. Another friend is having a heart surgery on this very day. The light and dark relentlessly weave their way into our lives; this reality is the joy of reading Seibert's fine-edged meditations. She is at her best when reminding us that we are not free to ignore what we have lost, for to do so is to miss God's presence with us at all times. With little warning, we are thrust into a list of the names of the children, teachers and shooter who died at Sandy Hook Elementary on December 14th. We are not free to forget, nor can we ignore the grief, for to do so does no honor to the unique and precious lives lost. Instead, the author claims this remembrance as a way to listen to the call of God and work toward non-violence. Seibert is our guide as we explore in her writings the real, the authentic, and the divine within the tangled and intricate lives we've been richly given. She makes us look unflinchingly at our response to God: What will it be today?"

—The Rev. Betsy Singleton Snyder is the author of *Stepping on Cheerios: Finding God in the Chaos and Clutter of Life.*

"Joanna is a master at captivating people's hearts. A gifted spiritual director, mentor and storyteller, she writes about the issues that truly matter through her mystical approach to the Christian faith. Her latest book, *A Daily Spiritual Rx for Advent, Christmas, and Epiphany* is a beautifully designed collection that gathers together her wisdom and insights on select passages from Scripture, books and poems. Her stories are interwoven with themes of longing, waiting, listening, honoring, forgiving, quieting, searching and being. In the spirit of this Holy season, find yourself in the stories and be grounded in mystery, silence and joy. From seekers to devout believers this is a book all Christians will enjoy and cherish."

—Catherine Miller is Spiritual Director, Retreat Leader, Ministry Consultant, Facilitator/Coach for *Invite Welcome Connect*.

"In *A Daily Spiritual Rx,* Joanna Seibert again offers spiritual seekers a way to be immersed in the teachings of our wisdom mothers and fathers, while inviting us to wake to God's presence in our daily lives during Advent, Christmas and Epiphany. Selections encourage us to recognize our own spiritual mentors who, on a daily basis, model the human struggle for faith, belief and goodness in this world. An excellent resource for both individuals and groups."

—Pan McCaslin, Mental Health Therapist and Spiritual Seeker.

A Daily Spiritual Rx
for Advent, Christmas, and Epiphany

Deanna
Bless you on your
journey through
Advent, Christmas, &
Epiphany. J

Joanna J. Seibert

Other books by Joanna Seibert

Earth Songs Press

A Daily Spiritual Rx for Lent and Easter

Earth Songs Press (Imprint: Temenos Publishing)

Healing Presence

The Call of the Psalms: A Spiritual Companion for Busy People

The Call of the Psalms: A Spiritual Companion for People in Recovery

Taste and See

Blessed Hope

Interpreting the World to the Church Vol. 1: Sermons for the Church Year

Interpreting the World to the Church Vol. 2: Sermons for Special Times

A Daily Spiritual Rx
for Advent, Christmas, and Epiphany

Joanna J. Seibert

A DAILY SPIRITUAL RX FOR ADVENT, CHRISTMAS, AND EPIPHANY

© 2019 by Joanna J. Seibert. All rights reserved. No part of this book may be used or reproduced in any manner whatsoever without written permission except in the case of brief quotations embodied in critical articles and reviews.

Library of Congress Cataloging-in-Publication-Data has been applied for.

Cover Art:
"Icon of St. Joanna the Myrrh-Bearer"
Uncut Mountain Supply
www.uncutmountainsupply.com
used by permission

Proceeds from *A Daily Spiritual Rx for Advent, Christmas, and Epiphany* will be donated to Hurricane Relief in the Central Gulf Coast and to Camp Mitchell Camp and Conference Center in Arkansas

Printed in the United States of America

To my younger brother, James H Johnson, Jr. Friends called him Jim or Bogie. His name is still Jimmy to me. We shared a great joy and excitement of Christmas from our youngest days. As his death occurred several years ago the day after Christmas, I always wonder if he were holding out for just one more Christmas!

An established author with over forty years of experience as a physician, minister, mother, retreat leader, and spiritual director, Joanna has collected daily messages from well-known spiritual authors and responds with a short discussion from her own experience as it relates to spiritual direction. *A Daily Spiritual Rx* should trigger a connection to God for the reader from her own experience to sustain her for the day. Joanna addresses the most common subjects and questions brought up by people on spiritual journeys or in spiritual direction as she shares books, readings, and experiences that have most connected her to God on her journey from both contemporary and classical writers.

Joanna is a frequent and well-known retreat leader and the multiple readings on varying subjects in the book are an excellent way to journey with readers on a retreat. The book could be part of curriculum in spiritual direction classes and schools, men's and women's church groups, pastoral care classes and schools. It also speaks to those in 12-

step recovery groups. Special writings address the liturgical seasons of Advent, Christmas, and Epiphany.

Table of Contents

Preparing for Advent
Arthur: Literature for Advent, Christmas, and Epiphany

God With Us

A Dog in the Manger

Watch for the Light

Advent
Sue Monk Kidd: Waiting

Sue Monk Kidd: Cocoons

Thomas Merton: Mary and Elizabeth 1

Mary and Elizabeth 2: Spiritual Friends

Resentments

Charleston: I Honor You, December 7

Guest Writer Isabel Anders: Advent, Awaiting the Child

Guest Writer Isabel Anders: The Tree of Life

Inside Voice

Buechner: Counter Culture

Holy Listening

New Word, Name

Icons

St. Lucy December 13

December 14

Hearing God

Earle: Julian

On a Pallet

Elizabeth's 111th Birthday

Gifts from Elizabeth

Celtic Spirituality: The Immanent Presence of God

Celtic Spirituality: Sacred Life of Hospitality in Community

Real World

Jesus: Light and Waiting

God Coming

Taylor: Learning to Walk in the Dark

Norris: Responding to Mystery, Advent 4

Buechner: Lord's Prayer, Advent 4

Mary and Joseph, Refugees

Christmas

12/24/1968 and Love

Buechner: Gift of Christmas

Boxing Day: Second Day of Christmas

Richard Rohr, Poe: Seeing on the Third Day of Christmas

Paying It Forward on the Fourth Day of Christmas

Brueggemann: Gift the Christmas Season on Its Fifth Day

Gesu Bambino

Buechner, Lewis: Telling Secrets on New Year's Eve

The Present, New Year's Day, Eighth Day of Christmas

Rohr: Low Point, Blue Christmas

Society of St. John the Evangelist: Offer Companionship on the Tenth Day of Christmas

Brueggemann, Benedict: Christians Living in the New Year

Rohr: Contemplation and Action

Epiphany

Meeting Epiphany

Charleston: Magdalene, The World Within

Thich Nhat Hanh: Walking Meditation

St. Francis: Hoeing; Gandhi: Dying

Blessing

Outrageous

Mosaic Community

Baptism

The Clark Fork River and Love

Benedictine Life

MLK: Racism, Inconvenient Time

MLK: A New Norm of Greatness

Grace, Flat Tire

De Mello: Selfish

Hibbs: Jesus Prayer

What Langley Knows

Merton: Prayer as Distraction

Kidd: Spiritual Whittling

Bolz-Weber: Spiritual vs. Religious

Charleston: Sacred Within Each of Us

Cloud of Unknowing

Nature's Voice

God Hole

Nouwen: Zero-Sum

Dreams

Hillesum: Answers

Kayla Mueller: God in Suffering

Waiting for God

Robert Johnson, Joyce Rockwood Hudson: Dreams Again

De Mello, Ignatius: Consciousness of the Past

Reading Again

Enneagram Retreat and Epiphany

Finding What Is Missing

Gerald May: Dark Night

May: Religion We Choose

May: Contemplative Prayer

Being with the Dying

Rohr: Good and God

Going Upstream

Non-anxious Presence/Or Less Anxious Presence

Temple: Church

Betsy Singleton: Living in Community at Home

Rohr: Service

Merton Epiphany in the World

Nouwen: Death

Balbir Mathur: Part of the Symphony

Lewis: The Great Divorce

Charleston, Nouwen: Tools, Movements

Silence, Waiting for Dolphins, Chant

Taylor: Spiritual Direction in the World

Addiction and Spiritual Direction

Charleston: Watched Over

Buechner: Meditation

Nouwen: Choosing Life

Palmer: Acquired Taste

Guenther: At Home in the World

Buechner: Spiritual Gifts

Nouwen, Merton: Meditative Prayer

Working Class Spirituality

Kelsey: Outreach

Keller, Tillich, Lamott: Faith, Doubts

Buechner: Surprise Visits

Nighttime Prayers, Compline

PREPARING FOR ADVENT

Arthur: Literature for Advent, Christmas, and Epiphany

"Many of us, when charting the timeline of our lives, can point to a moment when a story or poem happened."

—Sarah Arthur in *Light Upon Light* (Paraclete Press, 2014), p. 9.

Light Upon Light is a literary guide of daily and weekly readings and prayers by well-known authors for the liturgical seasons of Advent, Christmas, and Epiphany compiled by Sarah Arthur. She has also written similar companion guides for the long Pentecost season *(At the Still Point)* and for Lent and Easter *(Between Midnight and Dawn)*. Arthur emphasizes that this is not only a guide to prayer during a time of year that our lives become much too busy, but this is a literary guide to prayer. We all can remember and recall times when poems and Scripture and fiction moved us in our daily lives. Arthur believes that good literature can make a difference also in our lives when we most need it on a daily basis. The readings begin with the first Sunday in Advent and end the week of Ash Wednesday.

Arthur hopes to open up our imagination as she exposes us to brief excerpts or short works of writers well known to us as well as some authors we may not know but should! Arthur warns us that at some of the moments that we will encounter as we read this anthology, there should be an alert: "Warning: Powerful Spiritual Moment Ahead!" Arthur suggests that we read each reading not as something for our English Literature class or for pleasure, but as liturgical pieces for worship and especially prayer.

Each week begins with an outline for the week of an opening prayer, Scripture readings, readings from literature, a place of personal prayer and reflection, and a closing prayer to use for that week. Arthur suggests we now apply to poetry and fiction the ancient principles of *lectio divina* or divine reading that we have used in reading Scripture. We read the passage, meditate on it, pay attention to a word or phrase that connects to us, and finally we simply rest in God's presence. My experience has been to carry that word or phrase with me during that day or perhaps the whole week. Since this process is no longer being used for Scripture, she has christened it holy reading or *lectio sacra*.

I invite you to journey with me and with Sarah Arthur during the extraordinary seasons of Advent, Christmas, and Epiphany with an extraordinary spiritual practice of daily worship and prayer using well-known literature.

God With Us

"And the Word became flesh and lived among us."

—John 1:14.

I have used so many meaningful books to prepare for Christmas during the Advent season each year. I keep returning to *God With Us: Rediscovering the Meaning of Christmas,* first published in 2007 by Paraclete Press and edited by Greg Pennoyer and Gregory Wolfe. There are Scripture readings, essays by six well-known religious authors, and prayers, but what I most connect to are the paintings with each reading. Some days I only find time to look at the illustrations and say the prayer, but they both seem to stay with me. Eugene Peterson explains it in the introduction. "Over and over again they [artists] rescue us from a life in which the wonder has leaked out."

Other days I read everything including special essays about the meaning of the feast day of that week. I especially enjoy the readings during the twelve days of Christmas when the pace has slowed down and there is more time to digest what this smorgasbord feast of word and art presents to us. The book is now in paperback without the pictures, but if you can find the hardback, treasure it.

A Dog in the Manger

> "I want to put Jesus in the manger!"
> "You did it last year. It's my turn."
> "No, I'm the oldest, I get to do it."
> "Well, I'm the youngest, I think I should!"

—Jim Simons in *A Dog in the Manger and Other Christmas Stories* (Rowman & Littlefield, 2015), p. 1.

Jim Simons is an Episcopal priest who decides to write and tell a story for his Christmas Eve sermon every year, which eventually birthed into this collection of Christmas sermons called *A Dog in the Manger*. Simons reminds us that Jesus tells stories and the birth narratives consist of two different stories told by two authors, Luke and Matthew. He reminds us how the Christmas season is a special time to tell stories, stories about our roots, our parents and grandparents, and our early life.

Simons' stories are entertaining but with a deep and meaningful message of hope about the significance of the birth of Jesus, and especially the deep love of God for each of us. The stories are fiction but no doubt have been taken from his life experiences. The book's title comes from the first story about a puppy whose passion becomes going around town bringing back home to his new owner all the baby Jesuses from outdoor nativity displays.

I bought the book a few years ago when I was preaching more often and looking for material for sermons for the Christmas season. I often preach about Christmas pageants because I have been involved in so many, and at least half of Simons' stories are related to these dramas that always add some new and unexpected incarnational wisdom to Christmas.

This past year I have been reading a great deal of spiritual nonfiction writings in preparation for this book and two others. As Advent approaches I know I have been hungry simply for stories, and serendipitously this book appears in my stack for the Christmas season. My goal has been to read at least one story or at the least a half a story a day, but most days I find myself not being able to put the book down. Indeed, perhaps one factor for this craving has been the months I have put reading fiction on hold.

A Dog in the Manger has been exactly what I needed at the beginning of this liturgical year, and so I share it with you if by chance you are hearing a similar call.

Watch for the Light

"The spiritual Experience, whether it be of faith, hope or love, is something we cannot manufacture, but which we can only receive."

—Philip Britts, "Yielding to God" in *Watch for the Light* (Plough, 2001), p. 111-112.

Watch for the Light is a daily reading for Advent and Christmas by some of the best-known spiritual writers: Bonhoeffer, Dillard, Donne, Eliot, Hopkins, Kierkegaard, L'Engle, Lewis, Luther, Merton, Norris, Nouwen, Underhill, Yancy and many others. The short essays are three to five pages long, making each an Advent and Christmas reading that will take fifteen to thirty minutes to read and digest. This is a daily reading where we decide to devote a little more time to our Advent meditation with some of the most beloved spiritual writers. I am a major underliner, so I went back through the book to look for the most underlined essay. It was difficult since there were many underlined passages in every writing. One favorite was the essay "Yielding to God," by the British poet, Philip Britts. Britts writes that Mary's example for us of "let it be with me according to your word" is the essence of the Christmas story. Jesus is conceived out of surrender and born not out of "the head of Zeus" like Athena, but in a lowly stable with all the animals and the cold and the dirt.

Britts writes that Christ was born into poverty to heal the poverty of our hearts. Christ did not come as a moral tune up or as self-improvement guru or spiritual teacher. He came to show that the same breakthrough can occur in our hearts today just as " the word becoming flesh" changed the world more than 2000 years ago.

ADVENT

Sue Monk Kidd: Waiting

"Waiting patiently in expectation is the foundation of the spiritual life."

—Simone Weil.

I decided to read Sue Monk Kidd's book, *When the Heart Waits: Spiritual Direction for Life's Sacred Questions,* as a break from the intensity of the last book I studied, John Sanford's *Mystical Christianity: A Psychological Commentary on the Gospel of John;* but here again I am fooled. I have found myself underlining most of Kidd's book.

She reminds us of biblical waiters, Noah, Mary, Moses, Sarah, Jacob, Paul, the father and mother of the prodigal son—all who had to wait for God's answers for them. She reminds us of G. K. Chesterton's writing that praising and connecting to God is less a doxology, a short hymn of praise, than it is a paradoxology. The paradox is that we achieve the most and relate best to God by standing still!

When I visit with spiritual friends, I hope to offer Kidd's prayer of waiting, remembering Jesus' words to his disciples in the Garden of Gethsemane from Mark 14:32: "Sit here, while I pray." We only need to sit while Jesus prays for us, particularly the Jesus within us that will pray for us while we wait. If we are having difficulty doing this, Jesus reminds us of the community that surrounds us. Jesus is telling us to follow his example and ask friends to come and pray with us while we wait; and if we are that friend, to make the offer. We are also promised "a great cloud of witnesses" which is always around us, praying and waiting with and for us. Jesus reminds us that we do not need to wait and pray alone.

Sue Monk Kidd: Cocoons

"Our deepest struggles are in effect our greatest spiritual and creative assets and the doors to whatever creativity we might possess."

—David Whyte in *The Heart Aroused: Poetry and the Preservation of the Soul in Corporate America* (Crown Business, 2002), p. 62.

In *When the Heart Waits: Spiritual Direction for Life's Sacred Questions,* speaker and writer Sue Monk Kidd reflects on her spiritual journey at mid-life. She compares this journey to being in a cocoon of darkness and finally emerging as a butterfly. Even though this image is more often one of Easter, it can also be a model of our journey through Advent. In the cocoon, Kidd shares with us her experience of the false selves that keep us from being the person God created us to be—the defenses we use for survival that, like an addiction, eventually harm us. She reminds us to embrace them, kiss them, thank them for caring for us, but realize it is time to see what is beneath the thick skin cover-up.

Kidd describes the word crisis that in the Greek means separation, to leave the dead. Crisis is a holy summons to cross a threshold. Our response to crisis can be fighting it by looking for comfort or justice, or by waiting and using the time to be soul-making (the narrow gate). Instead of trying to ride the crisis she challenges us to attempt to understand and identify the feelings that come up in the crisis— like sorting tangled ribbons—and then express these feelings, especially through symbols. One such useful image is a cocoon, helpful in writing or sharing our story or reflecting on our dreams.

Those who are a part of a sacramental tradition in which everyday symbols such as water, bread and wine, and oil are used as outward evidences of a inner grace can identify with the use of earthly symbols in our spiritual lives.

Kidd talks about the difficulty of letting go by comparing it to the caterpillar's resistance to change, called "diapause." We fear leaving this former life as though it is "all we have." I personally experienced this "nothing left" as I heard a call to transition from my medical career.

Letting go also happens at retirement and when we find an empty nest after our children leave, or after we experience the death of a loved one. Kidd quotes from poet Rainer Maria Rilke that as we resist, we should try loving the questions in our heart like locked rooms or books written in a very foreign language. We should live the questions in the darkness, and the answers will come later, as we see resurrection. Jesus, of course, was the master of leading people to growth with more questions.

As Kidd moved from the cocoon of darkness to light, she began eastering or experiencing resurrection. She experienced delight in life, found a feminine side of God, learned a love of creation, and made a connection with her body. She learned that when she showed disrespect for her body, she also showed disrespect for the earth.

She also had a desire to live in the present, the *now here* instead of the *nowhere* when we live in the past or future, as though we are preparing to live instead of living. When we live in the present, time becomes not a straight line but a deep dot.

Kidd describes three stages of her contemplative awareness: first, hearing the words but not the music, then hearing the words and the music; and finally being the music.

Our orchestra seats for the Arkansas Symphony in Little Rock are almost on the front row. I wonder if these seats may be an unconscious icon and invitation to *be the music.* As we live in the present, listening to the music, we learn, as Kidd also did, little by little, about our authentic self, the true self—that musical piece God has made.

Thomas Merton: Mary and Elizabeth 1

"Then it was as if I suddenly saw the secret beauty of their hearts, the depths of their hearts where neither sin nor desire nor self-knowledge can reach, the core of their reality, the person that each one is in God's eyes."

—Thomas Merton in *Conjectures of a Guilty Bystander* (Doubleday, 1966), pp. 140-142.

Merton's mystical experience captures what spiritual friends seek to accomplish, seeing the light of Christ in each other. If only we could see each other as God does. I am reminded of the visit of Mary, the mother of Jesus, to her even more pregnant relative, Elizabeth, in Luke 1:39-56. As Elizabeth, carrying John the Baptist, hears Mary's greeting to her, the baby in her womb leaps for joy. Elizabeth is then filled with the Holy Spirit and greets Mary with the words: "Blessed are you among women, and blessed is the fruit of your womb." Mary then breaks into the song of praise and thanksgiving that we call The Magnificat: "My soul proclaims the greatness of the Lord." How wonderful, when we meet our neighbor, that the creative part within us, the Christ within us, leaps for joy to perceive the Christ within our neighbor. What does this story tell us occurs in our lives and the lives of our neighbor when this happens? We are filled with the Holy Spirit, and our neighbor is empowered to say or sing or live out The Magnificat.

Some of us are like Mary, just beginning to bear children. Many of us are like Elizabeth, beyond childbearing age. Some of us have never borne children; but this story of these two saints, along with Merton's story, still speaks to all of us. God is speaking to the birthing, the creative part of us that empowers us to see the Christ in ourselves and the Christ in our neighbor.[1]

[1] Seibert, *The Living Church,* May 25, 2003.

Mary and Elizabeth 2: Spiritual Friends

"When Elizabeth heard Mary's greeting, the child leaped in her womb. And Elizabeth was filled with the Holy Spirit and exclaimed with a loud cry, 'Blessed are you among women, and blessed is the fruit of your womb.' … And Mary said, 'My soul magnifies the Lord, and my spirit rejoices in God my Savior.'"

—Luke 1:41-47.

This visit of Mary to Elizabeth in Luke is one of our most descriptive Scripture passages about what it is like to be and have a spiritual friend or soul mate, seeking to see Christ in each other. The response by our neighbor may sometimes be just as miraculous as being able to respond with the joy of The Magnificat.

The story tells us that seeing Christ in our neighbor is a gift of the Holy Spirit. We are to put ourselves in position to receive this gift of the Holy Spirit; then see Christ in our neighbor; and then honor Christ in our neighbor. The Spirit enables us to look and listen for and honor the Christ in those we encounter. The promise of this story is that when we reflect the Christ in our neighbor back to him or her, he may also see the Christ in himself and be enabled to live out—and even sometimes sing out—The Magnificat.

What does it mean to "sing out The Magnificat"?

"My soul magnifies the Lord,
and my spirit rejoices in God my Savior,
for he has looked with favor on the lowliness of his servant."

The words are very clear. It is living out a life of gratitude and praise and being open to God working in our lives even in times of great stress. Our role model is an unmarried, pregnant young girl who is enabled by the love of her older relative to express her faith in her God so eloquently. The fruit of the Spirit that springs forth when we see Christ in each other is gratitude and praise. This is our sign that we are indeed open to honoring God in each other.

What a difference we could make in our own lives as well as our neighbors' if we could each be an Elizabeth to the Marys we daily visit at home and at work. When we see Christ in our neighbor we will find that our true self, our God connection within, will also "leap for joy"! [1]

[1] Seibert in *The Living Church,* May 25, 2003.

Resentments

"Resentment is like drinking poison and waiting for the other person to die."

—Attributed to St. Augustine and many others.

I have had a lot of experience with resentments in my own life. In addition, so many people come for spiritual direction because of resentments or harms done to them by other people. These resentments block us from a relationship with God as we obsess about what this person has done to us, thinking about this injustice more and more. The person or the event becomes our higher power, our God. There cannot be a relationship with God because so much of our existence is centered on what was done to us and how we can react or even cause harm to that person. My experience is that when I can calm down and have some realization that this person has taken over my thoughts and has indeed become my God, I slowly attempt a pathway to forgiveness. I don't want this person or situation to be my higher power, to take up so much space in my limited life.

The first step is praying daily for that person. Praying does not change the person that harmed us, but praying can change us.

One other observation can be helpful. We do not have far to look to see others whose resentments for harms done to them have taken over their existence. Some try to hide it. Some openly live a life of resentment. It changes who they are. Anger, bitterness, self-centeredness live in that body. Wholeness is excluded. Some become almost paralyzed by the resentment and cannot deal with life on life's terms. They in turn begin to resent others who do not appreciate the harm that was done to them. Addictions creep in as temporary harmful solutions to the increasing pain that the resentment brings. That person who harmed them is still hurting them. They live a very sad, isolated life, an icon of who or what we do not want to be.

Forgiveness is our only option if we want a relationship with God and a relationship with others.

Charleston: I Honor You, December 7

"I honor you. I honor you for who you are and for what you have done. You did not become the person you are without effort. You have weathered many storms and seen many changes. You have kept going when others might have given up. You have lived your life like an art, creating what you did not have, dreaming what you could not see. And in so doing, you have touched many other lives. You have brought your share of goodness into the world. You have helped more than one person when they needed you. I honor you, for walking with integrity, for making hope real, for being who you have become, I honor you."

—Bishop Steven Charleston, Daily Facebook Page, December 7th.

This past week on December 7th we observed the anniversary of the Japanese attack on Pearl Harbor. It was also the anniversary of the day I stopped smoking almost forty years ago. That was the day of my grandfather Whaley's funeral. He had taught me the most about unconditional love. I wanted to do something to honor him, and knew he so disliked my smoking because his mother had died of lung disease (Tuberculosis) when he was seven years old.

My grandfather taught me about love when he was alive and saved my life when he died. My younger brother died of complications from smoking, and I could so easily have done the same.

I honored my grandfather and his mother two years ago when my husband and my daughter helped me make the trek to my great-grandmother's grave in an isolated graveyard in the Great Smoky Mountains National Park. It was not an easy adventure. We entered the park, went over one small bridge on a dirt road, then an even smaller bridge; parked on a road with a chain across it; and walked a half-mile on an uneven path with roots crisscrossing it until we came to the secret, well-kept cemetery, a cathedral-like open space framed by a canopy of trees.

My experience with the grief recovery group, Walking the Mourner's Path, teaches me that honoring those you love who have died is one of the most significant ways of healing. So this week I do what others have taught me.

Anders: Advent, Awaiting the Child

"Isabel Anders wrote these Advent meditations while waiting for her first baby to be born. I read them in my husband's hospital room, watching him die. Now another Advent approaches, another time when birth and death draw close together and it is not always possible to tell which is which. As we move into Advent we are called to listen, something we seldom take time to do in this frenetic world of over-activity. But waiting for birth, waiting for death—these are listening times, when the normal distractions of life have lost their power to take us away from God's call to center in Christ."

—Madeleine L'Engle in her Introduction to *Awaiting the Child* by Isabel Anders.

Guest Writer: Isabel Anders

John the Baptist represents the call to radical preparation of one's whole life for the coming of the kingdom. His is an extreme message, and his own story ends in an early death. Yet while he lived, he praised the Lord with his whole being, his habits, his reputation, his life—for all it was worth. He brought the messages of the Old Testament prophets, especially that of Isaiah, into focus, and validated the hope expressed so long ago. A way, a path to God, would be prepared. A voice cries, "In the wilderness prepare the way of the Lord, make straight in the desert a pathway for our God" (Is. 40:3).

The call to repentance must always precede praise. Acknowledging sin clears the way for the truth of God's deliverance, for the Messiah to come into his own. And praise naturally follows the revelation of truth. John was the last forerunner of the Lord, a close earthly relation of Jesus. As a baby he had leaped in his mother Elizabeth's womb at the announcement that Christ would be born into the world, a foreshadowing of his prophetic mission to praise and acknowledge Messiah with his whole being.

The connection between repentance and praise that the Baptist exemplifies is a fitting one in Advent, helping us to hold the tension between joy-in-waiting and joy-set-loose. ...

In Advent we talk of preparing, of waiting, and therefore it would be almost impossible to avoid mentioning what it is we are waiting for, and why. Yet our emphasis on repentance, intermingled with praise, can sometimes give our songs a minor key. In these days we need to consider our own condition, and dare to think, "What if he had not come?" Our redemption hangs in the balance, and "all lies in a passion of patience" as we wait.

We pray that he will come to our hearts, as he did in the lives of those faithful believers: Mary, John, Anna, Simeon, Elizabeth. Acknowledgment of our own unworthiness, yet acceptance of the gift—two distinct actions—are as inseparable in us as they were in those saints. Our belief, like their hope, is part of the ongoing story of redemption. We are brought into line with the whole event through repentance and praise.

—From *Awaiting the Child: An Advent Journal* by Isabel Anders (Cowley, 1987, 2005)

Anders: The Tree of Life

"The tree of life, in God's plan, is more than a figure of speech. It is a description of the physical branching out of families, one way through which God's Word and his ways may be passed on. In this context, parenthood is both the most natural of callings and the most humbling privilege. It is important to remember how much God cares about physical life. For all my abstract thinking about images and ideas, my greatest task at the moment is to eat and drink properly to become a fit branch for the flowering of a new life. 'It is not the spiritual which is first but the physical, and then the spiritual,' Paul reminds us in 1 Corinthians 15:46."

—Isabel Anders in *Awaiting the Child: An Advent Journal* (Cowley, 1987, 2005).

Guest Writer: Isabel Anders

As the foreshadowing of Jesus' conception began with the first woman, and the promise was brought to fruition in Mary, so that tree, built through generations, out of the root of Jesse, is truly a Tree of Life, nurtured in the most human manner. Earthly lives and deaths are its tenuous branches, faithfulness and weakness are woven into its life, and God calls blessed those who choose to "abide" in him in order to bear the necessary fruit.

Human life, it seems, is never irrelevant to God's plan. Instead, we are in the thick of it. We can enter into this design, this story, by accepting the joys and pains of our humanity and submitting them to the good of the kingdom. We can rejoice that participation in its growth is allowed, and cooperate by choosing those things that build and sustain life for our families, our communities, our world. As Moses urged his people Israel in the crucial early stages of the tree's growth: "Therefore choose life, that you and your descendants may live" (Deut. 30: 19).

The tree has been a symbol of life from the very beginning. But we cannot forget that in the sweep of the continuing story, life and death converged on a tree—the cross of wood that both took Christ's earthly life and won our redemption into ongoing life. As the seed for the tree begins as a very small entity, yet carries in it all the potential for the flowering of the whole tree, so Advent carries in it the seed of the whole drama of our salvation. The planting, the watering, the tending can be conscious acts in our lives, as we wait for God to give the increase, to bring about his purposes in the world and in our lives—in this place, in this hour.

—Isabel Anders is the author of *Awaiting the Child: An Advent Journal* (Cowley, 1987, 2005) as well as Managing Editor for Synthesis Publications. Synthesispub.com

Inside Voice

"For whatever reason, God never seems to shout when trying to get my attention. God always uses his "inside voice," as my mother used to call it. Shouting, and calling, and crying out, and throwing people off their horses is great stuff, but that's not how I hear God. I hear God in a whisper; in a look; in a turn of the head; in a subtle expression on a face."

—Br. James Koester, SSJE, in "Brother, Give Us a Word," a daily email sent to friends and followers of the Society of Saint John the Evangelist, a religious order for men in the Episcopal/Anglican Church. www.ssje.org.

The irony here is that as we read this from Br. Koester about God speaking to us in God's inside voice, I am practicing preaching with all my might with my outside voice. My voice is soft. It is a legacy from my father who was soft spoken. It is a blessing and an impediment. It is a blessing as I talk to people and can more easily relate to them as a gentle listener. But when I stand in the pulpit to preach the word of God or speak out to a group, I have always had difficulty projecting that message even with good amplification. My husband always sits in the back of any congregation or meeting giving me signs that I need to increase my volume. I have spent years working with an amazing speech pathologist, but still have to push my voice. Anyone with a hearing impairment may have special difficulty hearing me.

My present rector has taken me on as a project, helping me learn to increase my volume. He let me read a prayer outside at a burial office as an "audition" to see if I had an outside voice. Yesterday I preached at a church without amplification. I felt as if I were shouting the whole time.

So what is the point of all this in reference to our relationship with God? For me, I am just acutely aware of what an inside voice sounds like and what my outside voice sounds like. My connection to God does indeed come in the form of an inside voice quietly slipping in. I also know we hear these soft messages at moments when we least suspect the voice of God, usually in interruptions of our daily routine.

God also seems to speak most clearly in Advent in an inside voice—while the world is more than ever blasting at us in outside-voice mode.

I am wondering, however, if God also speaks to us with an outside voice, and we just never hear it because we have come to expect only the inside, quiet connection.

Does God's outside voice also speak at the least expected times by least expected people we don't usually listen to—or maybe don't even want to listen to?

For the present, my best experience with God's outside voice is in my dreams. Eventually my dreams become louder, insistent, and messy if I don't pay attention to them.

Buechner: Counter Culture

"To love your neighbors when an intelligent fourth grader could tell you that the way to get ahead in the world is to beat your neighbors to the draw every chance you get—that was what this God asked, Paul wrote."

—Frederick Buechner in *Secrets in the Dark: A Life in Sermons* (HarperSanFrancisco, 2006), p. 199.

Buechner reminds us how countercultural the Christian faith was from the get-go as well as today. There is no better time to experience this than in the season of Advent in the Church Year. It is the four weeks before Christmas at the beginning of the Church Year. While during December our culture is hurrying, overloaded, frantic, caught up in a commercial craziness, the season of Advent calls us to a quiet preparedness, watching, waiting, pausing. In fact, the staff at our church has chosen "Pause, Breathe, Wait, Watching for the Christ child" as our theme for the season. *Pause, Breathe, Wait, Watching for the Christ Child.*

Advent is my favorite season, and this call to quietness makes it even more so. We put on pause the cacophony inside and outside of our heads, sit in a favorite chair, look or walk outside, light candles, feel something moving inside of our body as we move from our head to the rest of our body and become grounded in the present moment. The air we breathe in and out is full of the anticipation of new birth in us and in the world. The Christ child who is already within us wakes up and opens his eyes and smiles—as the Christ within us sees the light of Christ across the room in someone quite different from us whom we want to know better.

Holy Listening

"Listening creates a holy silence. When you listen generously to people, they can hear truth in themselves, often for the first time.."

—Rachel Naomi Remen in *Kitchen Table Wisdom: Stories That Heal* (Riverhead Books, 1996).

One of my partners at work gave me this book by Rachel Remen, another physician who writes about the spiritual life in the ordinary. I remember the book; but I also remember the kindness of the giver, and offer thanks for him and the times, often very holy, that we had together. I have learned that a book is meaningful to me not only for what is in it but for the person who gave me the book.

I think of Margaret Guenther and her book *Holy Listening: The Art of Spiritual Direction.* The message I keep hearing this Advent is to make part of my Advent discipline a holy listening to those with whom I do not agree. My husband and I, for brief periods of time, listen to a news program that we know will tell a different story than what we are used to hearing. How do those of us who hear so differently share what we have learned and then search together for the truth? I don't know that answer; but perhaps at least hearing a different story and a variant interpretation as to what is happening can help us understand why others believe what they do.

There is also another setting in which I am trying to be a holy listener. I frequently find myself with people who speak up too often, and sometimes have only what I feel to be boring words to offer. In the past I would cut them off and try to escape from the conversation.

During this season I have been trying simply to listen and listen for the Christ within them. One observation is that I have difficulty seeing and hearing Christ in them when I have lost my connection to the Christ within myself. It is the Christ, God, the holy, the Spirit within us that can make that precious contact. I think that understanding is our job. If we stay connected to the God within, we will discern the answers that we may hear in holy listening and enter into relationship with those with whom we have difficulty.

    I am holding on to this hope.

New Word, Name

"But Moses said to God, 'If I come to the Israelites and say to them, "The God of your ancestors has sent me to you," and they ask me, "What is his name?" what shall I say to them?' God said to Moses, 'I AM who I AM.' He said further, 'Thus you shall say to the Israelites, "I AM has sent me to you."'"

—Exodus 3:13-14.

Every day I try to learn a new word. My word for today is *splash stick*. Actually, it is two words. It is the green stick that Starbucks puts in your coffee cup to keep the coffee from spilling out of the hole from which you drink. For years we have called it the green stick, spill stick, the thing, the stopper, long green thing. But now, after so many years, we know its real name—or at least that is what the courteous Starbucks attendant or barista at the take-out window called it today. Barista was a new word for me several years ago. Splash stick is today. Splash stick, I will now honor you and call you by your proper name.

How important it is to be called by our correct name. There is something enriching in hearing our name called properly. It means we are real, a person. *We are known.* Someone may recognize our true identity. My name is Joanna, but sometimes people call me Joanne. I want to say, *I am not Joanne. That is the name of my friend who died.* I cherish my name because my parents chose it to honor two of my grandparents, Joe and Annie, who immediately began teaching me how to love.

Of course, Seibert is mispronounced so many ways. We have learned to accept what we are called with humor. Cebert is the most common pronunciation of this last name I was given as a gift from my husband's beloved family. We always know we are getting a call from someone who does not know us when a phone conversation begins with, "Hello, Mrs. Cebert."

As a result, I am now more sensitive to when I have called someone else by the wrong name—which now is happening more than I would like to say. When I slip, I detect an unrest in the previously peaceful air and a look of pain on the person's face, never completely concealed.

As for God, we know God's name only as "I Am." God doesn't seem to have this hang-up that we humans do of needing to be called by name. God just desperately wants us to love him or her or whatever and maybe say something. "I am mad at you, God. I am so thankful, God. I love you, God." All these seem acceptable. Spiritual friends suggest that maybe we don't really have to call God by name, but just sit and be present with God. This tells us a little about the difference in God's wisdom and ours.

Through an angel God does tell Mary and Joseph to give Jesus his name. I presume that God knew it would be hard for us to call Jesus by his name, "I Am."

So, what should we do? Perhaps we are to continue to call each other by name whenever we can and continue to try to comprehend the great mystery of God's love, so different from ours. Perhaps we are to strive to love as best we can and offer that love up to a God who someday may tell us God's name. Maybe instead, God will surprise us and give us another name as he did for Abraham, Sarah, Jacob, and Paul.

Maybe someday we may realize that our name is already several syllables or part of the "I AMS" written into the mysterious parts of God's name.

Icons

"I have always heard that icons represented 'windows into heaven,' glimpses of the glory of the life to come, hinted at in golf leaf and vivid colors suggesting fullness of life. But our speaker countered this view by pointing out that we don't really need 'windows' so much as eyes that are opened up to see what is around us here, in this life. For in Orthodox thought heaven is not so much 'another place' that needs to be peered into, but rather the quality of life in Christ which begins here through the power of his resurrection. In this view, eternal life includes the day-to-day getting there, the faithful journey of the saints as they are permitted glimpses of glory that punctuate everyday life, especially as they are revealed to us in corporate worship. No wonder Orthodox services tend to be so long—with seemingly endless choir responses and many opportunities to grasp the beauty and joy of resurrection, especially as it is celebrated in the season of Easter."

—Isabel Anders in *Awaiting the Child: An Advent Journal* (Cowley, 1987, 2005).

A recent short dream has called me back to a daily use of icons as my spiritual practice. In the dream the icons for my hard drive and my backup on my computer desktop have suddenly disappeared, but the icons for the documents I am working on are still there on my desktop. I have difficulty understanding that, as the desktop icons should not be there without the hard drive. My dream group and my spiritual director tell me that this may mean the hard drive and backup are still there but hidden. The things that I use for support, that I think I have lost, are still there but hidden.

One of the people in my dream group with extensive computer experience reminds us that icons are also called shortcuts. This offers a new understanding of icons. Computer icons help us more easily access information that is behind them. That is what icons on our desktop as well as religious icons do! Religious icons are shortcuts, often also called "windows" to connecting to God; but Isabel Anders tells us there is much more to it. They are also exercises in recognizing beauty and God, so that we can transfer that skill to realizing the presence of God all around us. So icons could also be considered spiritual *Cliff's Notes*—a concentrated experiential practice of awareness, connecting us to the kingdom here on this earth.

I hope my icon-loving friends will not view this as trivializing the spiritual practice of using icons. In fact, my own desk and walls are covered with many icons, so that everywhere I turn I can hope to connect to them. Icons help me stop in my busy day to remember what the day is all about.

All this is just my inadequate attempt to introduce to icons those who may be afraid to use them, thinking they signify foreign practices or idol worship.

Spending time with a favorite icon, especially one of Mary and Jesus, is a favorite Advent meditation of many spiritual friends.

St. Lucy December 13

"Santa Lucia, thy light is glowing
Through darkest winter night, comfort bestowing."

—Swedish Children's Folk Song.

Already today, this December 13 in the darkest hours of the morning (2 a. m. to 4 a. m.), in Sweden and Norway, the eldest daughter of a family—wearing a white gown, a red sash, and with a crown of lingonberry twigs and seven blazing candles on her head—emerges out of the darkness carrying a tray of rich saffron buns and steaming coffee, to wake up her family. Every village also has its own Lucy who goes from one farm to the next carrying a torch to light her way, bringing cookies and buns to each house and returning home by daybreak.

The winner of the Nobel Peace Prize for literature often has the honor of lighting the candles on the head of the "Lucy" for the city of Stockholm. Throughout Sweden, the feast day of Lucy is celebrated as a festival of lights, with bonfires rich with incense and candlelight parades. How in the world did this honoring of St. Lucy become so important in Scandinavia, when the original Lucy was a native of Sicily? The tradition of honoring Lucy may have taken hold in Sweden after Vikings who traveled south on peaceful trading expeditions to Italy brought back stories of the early Christian martyr, Lucia.

December 13 in our calendar is almost the shortest day of the year. Somehow the Scandinavians began to honor a young Sicilian girl, Lucy, whose name means "light," at a time during the darkest part of their year. It is all a mystery; but the tradition is beautiful.

I especially honor this day because two friends who carried the light of Christ to so many people died on this day seven years apart. Another light bearer who was our great teacher and friend is having major heart surgery today. So, in my own prayers on St. Lucy Day, I remember special friends who have brought light out of darkness to so many; but I especially remember those in my own life who showed *me* the light in times of darkness.

This is my Advent suggestion: for you to remember today, on St. Lucy Day, those who brought the light of Christ, the light of God, the light of the Spirit to you.

This is a special tradition that the Scandinavians have given us to remember the light that shines in our darkness. We can also carry the tradition to our homes. In the past, our family has often celebrated St. Lucy Day during the second week of Advent, with our oldest granddaughter serving buns at an Advent family service. She dresses in white with a red sash and carries a candle as we all say together the traditional song above, that Lucy sings on her rounds.

December 14

Remembering the names of children and teachers killed at Sandy Hook Elementary School on December 14, 2012.

"Holding these persons in our broken-open hearts, we are less likely to forget."

—"Advent Message for Today" from St. Mary's Cathedral, Memphis, December 10, 2018.

Charlotte Bacon, 6
Daniel Barden, 7
Olivia Engel, 6
Josephine Gay, 7
Ana Marquez-Greene, 6
Dylan Hockley, 6
Madeleine Hsu, 6
Catherine Hubbard, 6
Chase Kowalski, 7
Jesse Lewis, 6
James Mattioli, 6
Grace McDonnell, 7
Emilie Parker, 6
Jack Pinto, 6
Noah Pozner, 6
Caroline Previdi, 6
Jesica Rekos, 6
Avielle Richman, 6
Benjamin Wheeler, 6
Allison Wyatt, 6
Rachel Davino, 29 (Teacher)
Dawn Hochsprung, 47 (School Principal)

Nancy Lanza, 52 (Mother of gunman)
Anne Marie Murphy, 52 (Teacher)
Lauren Rousseau, 30 (Teacher)
Mary Sherlach, 56 (School Psychologist)
Victoria Soto, 27 (Teacher)
Adam Lanza (shooter)

"To forget the dead would be akin to killing them a second time." — Elie Wiesel.

The "Advent Meditation for Today" from St. Mary's Cathedral in Memphis listed the names of the children and teachers killed at Sandy Hook Elementary School six years ago. Elie Wiesel, renowned survivor of the Holocaust, will keep reminding us in his writings, which live on after him, that remembering those who have died, especially their names, helps us to keep them alive. We are called to keep their memory and the memory of so many others present in our hearts to remind us how the availability of guns and assault weapons is out of control in our country. These children and their teachers cry out to us to save the lives of the children they will never have.

As we long for peace this Advent, may we pray for courage and sacrifice and forgiveness and compassion and wise discernment—for solutions to this crisis for our country. May we be guided by what we can learn from so many other countries that have found answers to this issue.

So, what do the children and teachers of Sandy Hook Elementary School have to do with spiritual direction? The God of love daily calls us to spread the love we learn as we connect to the God within us and

God in our neighbor. We know our God grieves with all these children and their families, and we are called to connect to their grief in some unknown way as well. Out of our love and grief we are called to honor those who have died by working to prevent such acts of violence in the future. Discernment and action are just as important in the spiritual life as prayer and silence and contemplation and forgiveness.

Hearing God

"As we live in this season of Advent, awaiting the coming of the Lord, we might examine our hearts to see if they are truly open. Are we open to God speaking to us in the language of everyday events? Are we willing to hear God's admonitions and to accept God's guidance, or are we happier to justify our selfish behaviors and chart our own way in life? May the Lord find in us hearts that are open and ready to receive him, whenever and however he chooses to come to us."

—Br. David Vryhof in "Brother, Give Us a Word," a daily email sent to friends and followers of the Society of Saint John the Evangelist, a religious order for men in the Episcopal/Anglican Church. www.ssje.org

This is our daily question. Are we following our will or God's will? Are we listening to God or are we listening to ourselves and what promotes ourselves and our own self-interest? My experience is it is so hard to know, and I have learned to listen cautiously to those who tell us they know exactly what we are to do. I usually do not know if what I am doing is God's will until much later.

So, what do we do? We try to put ourselves in position to hear God's will. This means being silent, practicing spiritual exercises; dwelling in thin places where the spiritual and physical world seem to have only a thin membrane between them; living in community with other spiritual seekers who share experiences; studying Scripture and stories of those before us in our own religious traditions; worshiping in community.

My experience also is that when I feel or know the fruit of the spirit after discernment, this is a sign that I am being guiding by the Christ within, the Holy Spirit, the God of our understanding. (Galatians 5:22: love, joy, peace, patience, kindness, generosity, faithfulness, gentleness, and self-control.)

This is not a walk we do alone. We are surrounded by a cloud of witnesses who have traveled before us and who are now with us to guide us.

Earle: Julian

"Then, with a glad face, our Lord looked into his side, and gazed rejoicing; and with his dear gaze he led his creatures' understanding through the same wound into his side. And then he revealed a beautiful and delightful place which was large enough for all humankind who shall be saved to rest there in peace and love."

—Mary Earle in *Selections from Revelations of Divine Love by Julian of Norwich,* annotated and explained by Mary Earle, Long Text 24 (SkyLight Paths, 2013), p. 69.

Episcopal priest and well-known writer, Mary Earle, was the keynote speaker this year at the Community of Hope International meeting at Camp Allen, Norfolk, Virginia. Her topic was "Julian of Norwich and the Oneing Love of God." Julian was a 14th-century English mystic who is perhaps best known for her saying "All shall be well. All shall be well," as well as her Revelations of Divine Love, her reflections on a series of visions or showings she received when she was near death. The writings are in two parts—Short Text written soon after the visions and Long Text written much later—and are thought to be the earliest book written by a woman in Middle English.

We know so little of her life and even her name, except that in later life she became an anchoress to St. Julian Church in Norwich, living in a walled-off cell connected to the church. Julian lived in a difficult time before the Reformation, during the Hundred Years' War between England and France and through three outbreaks of the deadly Black Plague, caused by bacteria living in the fleas of rats, and decreasing the population of Europe probably by half. There also was a lack of leadership in the church with the Great Western Schism; sometimes there were two and even three popes.

All this is to say that most people must have felt as though the world was coming to an end! But in the midst of this comes Julian's message from her mystical experience—not with an angry God who must have retribution, but with the God of love. This God of love comes to her through her relationship and visions of the suffering of Jesus on the cross. Earle believes wherever Julian mentions Jesus she means the Trinity, God in three parts. Through God's suffering, Julian saw and felt God's love for all mankind.

Julian believed that we can enter into a mystical relationship with God through suffering, where, like the disciple Thomas, we enter into the wound in Jesus' side and find a place large enough for all mankind to rest in peace and love; or, like Nicodemus, we are born again through pain and suffering.

Earle suggests that instead of our arguing over how Jesus was born of Mary, our energy should be centered on whether Jesus' and God's deep love is being born in us.

This is our ministry as spiritual friends: to help others see not a vengeful, hall-monitor God, but the God of love calling and caring for us even in the darkest times. In the light of Julian's understanding, we stand beside our friends in their pain and suffering. This pain was and is also so well known by our God.

On a Pallet

"He suffered under Pontius Pilate, was crucified, died and was buried; he descended into hell. The third day he rose again from the dead."

—The Apostles' Creed.

Bishop Jake Owensby of Western Louisiana reminds us in his blog, "Looking for God in Messy Places," about the line in the Apostles' Creed where Jesus descended to the dead ("Unbearable," Looking for God in Messy Places, July 1, 2018; jakeowensby.com). Bishop Owensby's message is that our God goes to the places that seem like hell on earth to us. I also remember that our definition of hell is the absence of God. Perhaps the creed is telling us that even when we do not feel the presence of God, when life seems unbearable, God is still there.

When we are there "in hell," when we feel unlovable, when our health fails, when we lose our job, when our best friend dies, when depression lives not only in a cloud above us but flows in our bloodstream and in the synapses in our brain, this is a hard belief to remember.

During Advent many churches celebrate a Blue Christmas at which the church remembers those who have died and offers to God the grief of those who are still grieving. This is also a time for us individually to remember and reach out to those who still live in sadness.

This image of a loving, caring God must be written on our hearts during times when we feel connected to God and are dwelling in what seems like heaven—so that we can then carry that knowledge and feeling with us when our life descends into hell. This is still too hard.

We cannot depend on ourselves to remember how much God loves us. This is why spiritual friends around us are so needed. This is why God calls us to community. When we become paralyzed with fear and loneliness and pain, we need spiritual friends to carry us on that pallet through the roof to God, as friends once brought a sick man to Jesus. Otherwise life becomes too hard.

This is not the only answer, but it is the experience I have known best as my friends bring me to be cared for by the God of love of their understanding—until I am once again connected to the God of love and compassion I once knew. Then more will be revealed.

Elizabeth's 111th Birthday

"But Ruth said, 'Do not press me to leave you or to turn back from following you! Where you go, I will go; your people shall be my people, and your God my God.'"

—Ruth 1:16.

In August we celebrated my mother-in-law's 111th birthday. She died when she was 81. Our church tradition honors people on the day of their death. Our family still remembers those we love on their birthday. I think this is because we remember the ways we celebrated their birthdays—or maybe for some unknown reason their love, their presence seems closer to us on their birthday. My daughter and granddaughter are named for her. Elizabeth taught school, second grade, for more than forty years. Her class was called Happy Town. I keep wondering if any of her thousands of students remember her. They do not know that August 30th is her birthday.

I try to Google her to find out the exact day she died. I do not find her. There is no Google picture of her either. But my life was changed by knowing her: her acceptance of me, her love for her grandchildren. There are so many saints like Elizabeth who changed people's lives, many people's lives, but are unknown to many.

When Elizabeth died I remember asking her in my prayers to watch over our children like a guardian angel, and I promised I would care for her beloved husband Bob who was left behind. Well, Elizabeth did a much better job of watching over our children than I did caring for Bob.

Whenever our children were away from home, my prayers would be to Elizabeth to be with them. I know she truly was, reminding them in some way that they were loved, keeping them out of harm's way.

I do feel her presence today, telling me that *all shall be well, all shall be well.*

My prayer is that others may remember and honor the Elizabeth who encouraged them and taught them about the unconditional love of God, just as Mary's Elizabeth did for her.

Gifts from Elizabeth

"Each of us carries in his heart an album of lovely pictures of the past: memories of events that brought gladness to us. I want you now to open this album and recall as many of these events as you can."

—Anthony de Mello, "Exercise 18: The Joyful Mysteries of Your Life" in *Sadhana: A Way to God; Christian Exercises in Eastern Form* (Image Books, 1978), p. 71.

I am spending another morning feeling the presence of my husband's mother, Elizabeth. She and Robert's dad taught me how to love.

I look down as I write. I am wearing Elizabeth's engagement ring and wedding band. They are bonded together. When Elizabeth started showing signs of Alzheimer's, Bob gave her rings to my husband, Robert. He almost immediately forgot where he put them; in fact, we had decided that they were lost.

Then three years ago, when Elizabeth would have been 104, as Robert was looking for something in an old briefcase in his office, he found the rings. We talked about what to do with them. Should we break down the diamonds and give them to our grandchildren? Finally, he decided to keep them just as they are. Then, in the summer of Elizabeth's 106th year, on the patio of Trio's Restaurant, Robert got on his knee and asked if we could become engaged. He then gave me his mother's beautiful rings that he had had sized for me at Sissy's Log Cabin.

I had not received an engagement ring when we decided to get married. So now, in the 49th year of our marriage, I began to wear these beautiful rings that were worn by Elizabeth for almost that amount of time. In Advent we remember the wisdom of waiting. Elizabeth's rings are an icon for me about waiting.

Did I remember to tell you that Bob and Elizabeth were married the same day, the same year as my parents?

So, what does all this have to do with spiritual direction? I think it is important to remember those who mentored and loved us. De Mello tells us to keep these times in an album in our imagination that we can repeatedly return to. I think we can still feel that love even long after they have died. Their love is with us or beside us or in us. I do not know exactly how it happens. These are the people who give us a little glimpse of the love of God. Often wearing a piece of a loved-one's jewelry or having something nearby that was precious to that person helps us connect to him or her.

We remember and give thanks for loved ones who are gone, especially as we approach Christmas and remember the joy and love they brought to our lives during this season. We are called now to honor them by passing on that joy and love to others.

Celtic Spirituality: The Immanent Presence of God

"Deep peace of the running wave to you,
Deep peace of the flowing air to you,
Deep peace of the quiet earth to you."

—Gaelic Blessing from *Carmina Gadelica*, 1900.

In Celtic spirituality, God's presence is perceived to be in and throughout the created world. There is no dualism. Nothing is seen as secular. All is holy. Nature is sacred. God's presence and handiwork are seen everywhere; but this was not pantheism. The hills, the sky, the sea, the forests are not God—but their spiritual qualities *reveal* God and are connected to God. This relationship is similar to the artist's connection to his painting. A painting or a statue, while bearing the evidence of the artist's hand, still has an existence separate from the work.

Gaelic Blessing was the John Rutter anthem our choir sang at my ordination. Since an early age, I have experienced what the words and music are communicating. As I sit by my desk, even in front of a picture window, I become consumed with my world and its problems and tend to become self-absorbed. I go outside, and it is as if I am in a different world. I suddenly experience a world larger than my own—a sacred one I did not create. My problems become small. I am connected to something beyond myself.

Following the moon rise at night, or the rising of the sun in the morning, or its setting in the evening—or listening to the constant rhythm of the waves by the ocean—brings a peace to my body and soul and mind that no drug or substance can duplicate. Nature helps us live in the present. This is where God meets us.

Authors to read to discover more about Celtic spirituality are John Miriam Jones, *With an Eagle's Eye,* 1998; Phillip Newell, *Celtic Benediction,* 2000, and *Christ of the Celts,* 2008.

Celtic Spirituality: Sacred Life of Hospitality in Community

"I sought my God;
My God I could not see.
I sought my soul
My soul eluded me.
I sought my brother
And I found all three."

—Ancient Celtic prayer.

In the tradition of Celtic hospitality, God is present not only in nature, but also in our neighbor, in ourselves, and especially in the stranger. This is a sacredness in relationships. I am told there is no word in the Irish language for private property. Faith is lived in community with a combination of periodic seclusion along with community and mission. *Anamchara* or soul friends (or spiritual friends or spiritual directors) are important relationships. Women are regarded as equals, and communities are not hierarchical. Monasteries rather than parishes are the basic components of the Church. The Celts value education, art, and music.

We made two trips to Iona off the western coast of Scotland, and would go back again in a heartbeat. You really do have to want to go there, though—traveling by ferry, down a one- lane winding road, and finally walking onto the small, three-mile-long island in the Inner Hebrides where Columba brought Celtic Christianity to England in

563. This is where the breathtaking illuminated manuscripts of The Book of Kells are believed to have begun to be written at the end of the 8th century. Iona is believed to be the site of an especially "thin" membrane between the spiritual and the secular. This was our experience as well. You walk a lot; eat good food; worship outdoors as well as in the ancient abbey and in a decaying nunnery; listen to the wind and waves; study high crosses; wear warm clothing, and watch the sea change the color of the 2,000 million-year-old rocks by the shoreline.

I often meet with spiritual friends who describe what is actually Celtic spirituality, though they have no name for it. This seems to be a sign of the universality of this type of spirituality. Again, we recommend Philip Newell, *Celtic Benediction;* and John Miriam Jones, *With an Eagle's Eye.*

Learning more about Celtic spirituality can be a natural journey for Advent.

Real World

"Often, as we conclude a retreat at Dayspring, someone will say: 'This has been powerful. I hope I can hold onto it back in the real world.' But the 'real world' is not the one to which we are going. We return to the 'unreal' world where the culture is distorted and trapped in pretense. The 'real' world is the one we were just in, where our hearts were opened and we gave inner consent to rest in God."

—N. Gordon Cosby, "Seized by the Power of a Great Affection: Meditations on the Divine Encounter" (Inward Outward, 2013). Inwardoutward.org

What an amazing concept Gordon Cosby, the founder of Church of the Saviour in Washington, D. C., brings to us this morning, late into Advent. *Real* means something is not artificial or an imitation. Real is genuine, not fake. *Unreal* is not living out of our true self, our core of love, the divine within us. Seeking power over others is artificial. Connecting to God, the power greater than ourselves, is real. Humility is real. Arrogance is posing as something we are not. Holding a newborn baby in our arms is real. Having that child we love taken away from us is unreal. The white sands of the Gulf are real. Oil stains on the beach are unreal.

Living with the fruit of the Spirit, peace, joy, kindness, patience, faithfulness, goodness, gentleness, self-control (Gal. 5:22-23) is real. Living in fear is living in an artificial world, another world, not the real world that God made.

This is a constant message from Jesus. "It is I; do not be afraid," is Jesus' message to his disciples as he walks on water toward them in the midst of a storm on the Sea of Galilee (John 6:20). "Fear not" are the first words all the angels from God proclaim. These were the first words to Mary. That's how we suspect the presence of angels, and even God, when we hear these words. Making choices out of fear is not real. It is not the world of the God of my understanding.

Phillip Newell frequently writes that a major premise in Celtic spirituality is that our core is good, that it is love, as opposed to Western or Mediterranean spirituality telling us that our core is sinful. So many of us live a life behind masks to seek to hide our sinfulness. At other times we become so overcome by our sinfulness that we are paralyzed—we live in a mechanical trance, going through the motions. This is not a real life. We have become disconnected from the love within us as well as the love of God and our neighbor.

So what do we do? We change the world and ourselves by concentrating on the core of love within us, the Christ within us—by trying to put ourselves in position to know that love. For many this means learning to live by a rule of life. We begin by trying to connect and spend time with our loving God. We try to love one person at a time, including ourselves.

When we are confronted with fear, we say our prayers. My mind keeps reciting the old saying, "Courage is fear that has said its prayers." The answers will come. We will begin to know and desire only what is real. It goes by the name of love.

Jesus: Light and Waiting

"I am the light of the world. Whoever follows me will never walk in darkness but will have the light of life."

—John 8:12.

Nestled away in the side chapel of Keble College, Oxford, is this haunting painting, "The Light of the World" by Holman Hunt. I stumbled on it on an adventure walk at Oxford one summer when we spent two weeks at nearby Wadham College. I was mesmerized by it and sat and visited it almost every afternoon. Hunt painted it in 1854 and sold it to Thomas Combe, who on his death willed it to Keble College. When Hunt heard that Keble was charging admission to see it almost fifty years later, he painted another picture four times larger with the understanding that it would be considered a "sermon in a frame." The much larger work went on an international tour of evangelism, in which hundreds did indeed become believers.

When I found out that this larger version was donated to St. Paul's Cathedral, I knew we needed to go back to London to see it, behind the altar in the North Transept, Middlesex Chapel. This version is just as haunting, but it is much harder to meditate on the painting with the crowds around it there. I was almost always alone at the chapel at Keble.

This is just a reminder of how art—even one painting—can make such a difference in the world. The figure of Christ, with his searching eyes, stands with a lantern on the other side of a door that is overgrown with dead weeds. There is rotten fruit on the ground. This speaks to me volumes more about our relationship with Christ than do most theological writings. Christ has been there for some time. No matter where we stand or sit in relationship to the painting, Christ's eyes are looking directly at us. The door in front of him opens from the inside. Christ is not banging on the door but persistently and gently knocking.

In Advent we are searching for the Christ child. Hunt tells us he is very near, knocking at the door of our hearts.

I give copies of this image to spiritual friends, especially when they are grieving God's absence. God is there waiting.

God Coming

"When he saw that they were straining at the oars against an adverse wind, he came towards them early in the morning, walking on the sea. ... But when they saw him walking on the sea, they thought it was a ghost and cried out, for they all saw him and were terrified. But immediately he spoke to them and said, 'Take heart, it is I; do not be afraid.' Then he got into the boat with them and the wind ceased. And they were utterly astounded, for they did not understand about the loaves, but their hearts were hardened."

—Mark 6:48-52.

During Advent we await and look for the coming of Christ in our hearts and lives. This has been my experience. God often comes to me in the early morning if I take time to get up and listen and read, or just look or sit outside. God comes when I am "straining at the oars against an adverse wind." God comes to me in some miracle, almost as if Jesus was walking on water again. It might be a word, a letter, an email, a call from someone through whom I would least expect to hear God's word. I "by chance" meet someone who was not on my agenda for the day.

God may speak in our daily Scripture reading. God may be the wind at my side, or the sun bringing light to the cold dawn, or the first bloom on a barren tree. I usually perceive God as a ghost and do not recognize the occurrence as a message from the one who cares so much for me. I may ignore it because it was not in my busy plan for the day. I may even cry out. I may be terrified by what I hear or see.

Talking to spiritual friends helps us see God in these places, whereas before we were blind to God's presence. I remember that if I somehow stay present to the moment and say my prayers, fear will leave me. Fear is afraid of prayer.

God literally gets "into the boat" at a point where my life is sailing on, and then the storm in my mind and in my body miraculously ceases. I am astonished. I do not realize why I am comforted, for my heart is still hardened. This happens daily. God does not give up on us and our hard hearts.

Taylor: Learning to Walk in the Dark

"God has done some of his best work in the dark, including resurrection."

—Barbara Brown Taylor in *Learning to Walk in the Dark* (HarperOne 2015).

The title of Barbara Brown Taylor's book, *Learning to Walk in the Dark,* itself describes a discipline to consider for Advent. I have learned so much from Barbara Brown Taylor. I read her first book, a collection of sermons on the Gospel of Matthew, *The Seeds of Heaven,* in a book group in the 1980s. I was magnetized by her use of words and her intimate Gospel message. She taught me how to be a narrative preacher, seeing God in the stories of the Bible and how these stories are true in our lives.

For years, I have gone to every conference she has led about preaching and writing, especially at the College of Preachers at the National Cathedral and Kanuga. I have read almost everything she has published that I could get my hands on. In recent years, she has taught me about seeing God in the world, pluralism, recognizing God in people of other faiths, seeing God in the dark. Finally, she has taught me to be me, not a Barbara Brown Taylor copy—but to find my own voice and be the person God has created me to be.

This is our job as spiritual friends, to help each other become the person God created us to be, not what we think our parents or children or spouse want us to be—not even to become the person we most admire. However, considering which people we look up to may give us a clue about some of the qualities hidden in us that are a part of the person God created us to be—and we should daily be grateful to them for it.

Norris: Responding to Mystery, Advent 4

"Mary proceeds—as we must do in life—making her commitment without knowing much about what it will entail or where it will lead."

—Kathleen Norris in *Amazing Grace: A Vocabulary of Faith* (Riverhead Books, 1998), p. 77.

The heart of spiritual direction and the spiritual life indeed is responding to mystery, and certainly Mary is our icon for responding to something that is a mystery to her and all of us to this day. First of all, we must be open to the presence of a call to mystery. I have sometimes imagined other young women that Gabriel visited who responded to the angel by saying, "Let me think about it"; "Come back later"; "This is really not a good time for me to do this"; "No, definitely, not!" or "You must be kidding!" (Of course, I always must explain to my dear Catholic friends that this is just a mind trip, an exercise in my imagination.)

There is no question that our answers to the mystery will change us and our life forever. My experience is that we can learn to respond to the mystery first in small ways so that when a larger call to the mystery comes, we are ready. This is the practice of awareness and openness. We must also be open to going off—or at least temporarily abandoning—our agenda and listening to the interruptions in our life. The mystery is all around us, in every waking moment, in nature and in young children, in older adults, often those in need and poverty, and especially in our interruptions.

Taking time to be in silence or with others in need or going outdoors each day can expose us to the mystery of a world greater than ourselves. Spending time with young children can connect us to joy and love without conditions. Some of the most spiritual people I know are older men and women who know better than any of us how little control we have in our lives and have accepted it and made peace with it.

The people I sit with who come to our food pantry often talk about how blessed their lives are. They see blessings in every offering. I learn from them that "Let it be with me according to your word" (Luke 1:38) can be one of our best mantras.

Buechner: Lord's Prayer, Advent 4

"In the Episcopal order of worship, the priest sometimes introduces the Lord's Prayer with the words, 'Now, as our Savior Christ hath taught us, we are bold to say ... '"

—Frederick Buechner in *Whistling in the Dark* (HarperSanFrancisco, 1988), pp. 83-84.

Buechner is reminding us of how bold we are to say the most recited Christian prayer. Of course, it is not really just a Christian prayer, since it was written by a Jewish rabbi telling other Jews how to pray.

My experience is that whenever I visit the sick or homebound or those in need, no matter what their mental state, they say or show some awareness of the Lord's Prayer. I have seen some, who seem unresponsive, twitch or move a hand or mouth a word or have a change in cardiac rhythm—or even begin praying when we close our visit with this prayer. Having once memorized and prayed this prayer is powerful, and could turn out to be one of the last parts of our memory to leave us.

Buechner, however, is emphasizing the prayer's boldness. If only we could find in our lives a little of what we are praying for in this prayer, the world would be dramatically changed, "turning our lives and our wills over to the care of God," as those in 12-step programs pray daily. This is similar to what Luke quotes Mary as saying in her response to Gabriel: "Let it be to me according to your word" (Luke 1:38).

How bold that we ask for forgiveness as we are forgiven. If we have any hope of being forgiven, we must extend the same grace.

How bold that we ask to be delivered from evil. I sometimes share that I recently was prepared to do something that my gut told me was not right, and some circumstances not of my own making kept me from it. It was an answer to prayer. God was doing for me what I could not do for myself.

When spiritual friends ask how to find God, I have suggested that they pray the Lord's Prayer boldly, as part of a rule of life, at designated times during the day that work best for them until we meet again. I will do the same, and we can compare notes.

Mary and Joseph, Refugees

"As I ponder what these last few days before the Nativity might have meant for Mary and Joseph, I can't help but see the connection between their journey to Bethlehem and flight to Egypt with the travels of so many refugee families searching for a new, safe home."

—Judith Schelhammer, Episcopal Diocese of Michigan.
www.edomi.org

My heart goes out to the many refugees in our world, especially those at our borders, who are just seeking basic safety for their own lives and their family. I also have become acquainted with several DREAMERS, undocumented young people who came with their parents years ago and now are seeking education and status. Their situation is very tenuous. This is the country they know and have grown up in. They have no connection to their country of origin. We would be deporting some of the hardest working groups of people I have known, people who already enrich and broaden our culture.

I try to connect to them in some small way by remembering that all of our ancestors were at one time refugees in this country, unless we are Native Americans.

I can also see ourselves in our search for God as refugees—often deciding to leave a place or point of view where we began, now seeking a wider, larger view of God, or a whole new life. Often this journey entails learning a new language. We step out on roads less traveled.

This, as well, cannot be an easy pathway. It is definitely a sacred adventure on which guides can be helpful.

CHRISTMAS

12/24/1968 and Love

"But the greatest of these is love."

—1 Corinthians 13:13.

If you were alive on December 24, Christmas Eve, 1968, to see the picture from Apollo 8 of the earthrise, do you remember what else you were doing? I remember much but also remember so little. My husband and I were interns at John Gaston City of Memphis Hospital, and working that night, so we missed the traditional Christmas Eve services. Instead we went to the quieter Christmas Day services at St. Mary's Cathedral that next morning. We were not married until the next year; but it was a special Christmas, the first holiday we were able to be together.

I do not remember the patients I took care of that night, or what presents we gave each other for Christmas. I do remember that our best friend, Charles Stallings, taught us how to make gold and red Christmas ornament balls that we hung on that first tree. We still have some of the large balls; and we try to tell our grandchildren, Zoe and Turner, about them as they traditionally help us hang them—or occasionally have fun literally tossing the decorative balls onto the upper limbs of our tree each year.

The most memorable part of that first Christmas, however, was that I was invited to meet Robert's parents for Christmas dinner that night at their home. I don't remember what we ate, but I do remember the red dress I wore. I was so nervous. I was damaged goods, and I feared that they would not be able to like, much less love me. I had been divorced, and Robert was in the process of being divorced. I remember how they accepted me with open arms and treated me as a lovable person from the start. Their unconditional love and care never ended. I still feel their presence today, even though they have been dead for some time.

The only way I can continue to return that love is pay it forward today to my children and their children and their spouses' families. I remember when Elizabeth died, I would pray that if she would continue to watch over her grandchildren, I would care for her husband, Bob. I didn't keep up my part of the bargain as well as she did. I could always have done more.

I know that love never dies. Bob and Elizabeth have taught me that. Today, almost fifty years later, I still feel the unconditional love they showed to me in so many ways. It is a presence. It is a feeling. It is knowledge. It is present in their only son, who also knows much more about unconditional love than I do. I also see it in their three grandchildren, whom they loved so dearly. I know love can change the world, one person, one family at a time. I have seen it.

Buechner: Gift of Christmas

"Be born among us that we may ourselves be born. Be born within us that by words and deeds of love we may bear the tidings of thy birth to the world that dies for lack of love. Amen."

—Frederick Buechner, "Come and See" in *Secrets in the Dark: A Life in Sermons* (HarperSanFrancisco, 2006), p. 55.

The gift of Christmas is the Incarnation, a big word that means that God loves us so much that God came among us and became human. It was and is a gift. The gift of the incarnation also extends to us, as it did to Mary. There is a part of God born in us and in every other person we will meet.

Advent is a time for us to prepare to honor the Creator by learning how to continue to unwrap that gift that we will celebrate receiving during the Christmas season.

My granddaughter and I have a tradition of spending time together wrapping presents, beginning in October. Wrapping gifts that soon will be unwrapped becomes a significant part of my year during this time.

As I meet with people in spiritual direction I cannot help but imagine how they are unwrapping that gift of the Christ child in themselves. We as spiritual friends have the privilege of watching and waiting with them for the excitement of Christmas morning. When some realize that Christ is in them, they excitedly unwrap the present, almost tearing the paper apart. Others unwrap the gift slowly and cautiously.

We as observers also receive a gift, for the gift of the Christ child is too powerful to keep and must be shared. Spiritual friends help us unwrap the gift in ourselves as well. The gift that now shines so brightly in them assists us in unwrapping that gift of the Christ child in ourselves.

All of our experiences are different, but the gift is continually offered to all of us by the One whose name is Love.

Boxing Day: Second Day of Christmas

"But the souls of the righteous are in the hand of God, and no torment will ever touch them."

—Wisdom 3:1.

My experience is that those who have known the death of a loved one around Christmas may have trouble finding the holidays to be a joyful time.

My brother died in December four years ago, in 2014 on Boxing Day, the second day of Christmas. He died less than four months after his 70th birthday, at almost exactly the same age that our father died. My brother was born on Labor Day and died on Boxing Day. We will have to work on the significance of all that.

Boxing Day is the day after Christmas, when servants in English households traditionally receive a gift in a box from their employer; and of course Labor Day honors those who are working and gives them an extra day of rest. I do know Jim loved Christmas. My brother also died on the day our Church Calendar honors Stephen, the first deacon and martyr. I don't know about a martyr, but my brother was definitely a survivor. He had open-heart surgery, three cancers, and at least three strokes.

Shortly after my brother died, I did something I have never done before. I prayed to ask him what he would like for us to say about him. I have given many funeral homilies, but never had prayed that question directly to the person who died. I now wish I had. This is what immediately came to me that my brother said: "I tried to be a good man, and I loved my family."

"I tried to be a good man, and I loved my family." So that was my message from my brother. I know he dearly loved his family and was very proud of his three sons. He loved his community, serving faithfully as a banker, a mentor for the Boys' and Girls' Club, and a member of the school board.

I know my brother especially loved his church, where he served faithfully.

Since the Episcopal Church is a love we both shared, we talked about it often. Only once did we have the privilege of serving at an altar together. That was at our mother's funeral, where we both were Eucharistic ministers serving the chalice.

My brother was an eight o'clock churchgoer. They are a different breed, a little more private, a little quieter, sometimes a little more reserved. They get the ear of the rector after the service, as there are so few people present that early.

My brother loved serving on the vestry, another rare breed. If an eight o'clocker is a lector or Eucharistic minister, he or she serves more often than do those at the later service. I tried to talk my brother into becoming a deacon, which I think could have happened if he had had a little more time. The Church is in the genes of our family. Our service comes out in many different forms, but we cannot escape it.

My brother was a believer, and there is no doubt that he now lives in the resurrection, just as he experienced so many resurrections in this life.

So today I am sharing with you some memories of my brother, my only sibling. I daily miss him, especially on holidays. I remember how when we were children we would wake up in the early morning on Christmas, too excited to sleep, and lie together in bed hoping by some miracle that our parents would wake up early. He so loved Christmas. I honor him by sharing Christmas stories about him and celebrating the holiday as he so loved to do. He always brought joy to my life, and I hope to keep sharing that joy, especially at this time of the year. Sometimes when our family is sharing stories I can hear his distinctive laugh, and I give thanks for our life together.

Richard Rohr, Poe: Seeing on Third Day of Christmas

"Most people do not see things as they are because they see things as *they* are."

—Richard Rohr, Center for Action and Contemplation. Adapted from *Everything Belongs: The Gift of Contemplative Prayer* (Crossroad, 2003).

Edgar Allen Poe also gives us more clues about seeing in his story "The Purloined Letter." In it, the Paris chief of police asks a famous amateur detective, C. Auguste Dupin, to help him find a letter stolen from the boudoir of an unnamed woman by an unscrupulous minister who is blackmailing his victim. The chief of police and his detectives have thoroughly searched the hotel where the minister is living, looking behind the wallpaper and under the carpets, examining tables and chairs with microscopes, probing cushions with needles, and finding no sign of the letter. Dupin gets a detailed description of the letter and visits the minister at his hotel. He complains of weak eyes so he can wear green eyeglasses and disguise his eye movements as he searches for the letter. There it is in plain sight—in a cheap card rack hanging from a dirty ribbon. He leaves a snuffbox behind as an excuse to return the next day and switches out the letter for a duplicate.

Rohr is calling us to put on a new pair of glasses, perhaps 3-D glasses, to see the depth of what is in plain sight around us in the present moment. We will meet God in this encounter. This is the call of the Christmas season.

Paying It Forward on the Fourth Day of Christmas

"It is important that we learn humility, which says there was someone else before me who paid for me. My responsibility is to prepare myself so that I can pay for someone else who is yet to come."

—Maya Angelou.

At Christmas, I often remember special friends who have died. I remember Sylvia, whom I dearly loved for many years. We worked together early in my ministry, and she taught me about servant leadership. She was a single mom, a nurse, and a caretaker like none other. She was a visitor from our church to the sick to say prayers; but she became more like a parish nurse as a medical advocate in connection with the hospital. Sylvia would go to nursing stations and let anyone there know what "her patients" needed.

We started a 12-step group at our church, which lasted for only about four months; but Sylvia was one of the first people who came to it. Afterwards she was in recovery for the rest of her life. We always believed we started it just for her and never regretted the effort we put into it.

Sylvia loved us—but more than us, she loved her grandchildren, whom she talked about almost constantly. She died too early while her grandchildren were still young. Somehow I stay connected to her family and know a little about her oldest granddaughter. I intermittently write to Darcy and tell her some of the stories about her grandmother; but I especially tell her how very much she was loved and adored by Sylvia. I honestly believe that Sylvia has in some way still been "suggesting" that I do this, the way she made "suggestions" so effectively in her physical life. This is exactly what she would tell me to do if she were physically beside me. Sylvia wants her granddaughter to know how much she was and is loved; and in turn, Sylvia is reminding me that I have an opportunity to do the same.

When I remember Sylvia's untimely death, I am moved to call or text or email or visit with my own grandchildren and remember what a privilege it is to let them know they are loved.

This was my Christmas present this year from Sylvia and will be for many years to come.

Brueggemann: Gift of the Christmas Season on Its Fifth Day

"Christmas is especially for those of us whose lives are scarred and hurt in debilitating ways. Of course, that means all of us. Christmas is about a word from God addressed to the world in its exhaustion."

—Walter Brueggemann in *Celebrating Abundance: Devotions for Advent* (Westminster John Knox Press, 2017), pp. 68-69.

So much of our life has been connected to schools and colleges. The twelve days of the church's Christmas season and especially the time between Christmas Day and New Year's Day is traditionally a slow-down time for higher education since people are on vacation or are less busy. It is amazing how my body and my mind have been conditioned over the years to live at a different pace during the Christmas season. It is a Christmas gift. The days are shorter. I can sleep until seven a. m. and go to my window and still watch the world yawn and wake up around me.

This morning is rainy and wet with a dense fog. There are fewer leaves. Even through the thick mist, I can see at a greater distance with a wider world view. I watch the deer gallop away together by my window—back to the woods as they hear the sound of cars. The busy territorial squirrels chase each other up and down trees. The cardinals and woodpeckers come to the feeder by my window to share space with smaller birds whose markings I cannot read.

I have time to listen to the rhythm of the rain. It is as hypnotic as ocean waves; but the ocean is like a Souza march keeping perfect time, while the rain changes and is slower and then faster, and then softer, and then louder like the improvisation of jazz.

I switch gears and, turning inside, I open my memory book to Christmases in the past, reenter those scenes and bring them alive again. Traveling to the beach. Shopping with children and grandchildren. Going to movies. Ice-skating. Family dinners. Watching slides. Eating leftovers. Reading new books, or old ones I keep in a to-read stack by my desk and bed. Writing. Visits to and from family members we have missed seeing during the year. Spending time with old and new friends I have neglected because of my busyness. Resting.

The Church Year gives us a few more days at the end of our calendar year for this short Christmas season, and extends it through Epiphany, the celebration of the arrival of the Wise Men on January 6. My prayer today is that I will open this gift and treasure the precious present of these twelve days of the Christmas season.

Gesu Bambino

"Upon a winter night,

Was born the Child, the Christmas Rose,

The King of Love and Light.

The angels sang, the shepherds sang,

The grateful earth rejoiced."

—Italian Children's Christmas Carol

As I remember how my younger brother died several years ago on the day after Christmas or Boxing Day—or the Feast Day of St. Stephen—I still miss him.

On the last Sunday in Advent, Advent 4, the day before Christmas Eve, as I was preparing in the early morning to go to the eight o'clock service, I heard on our National Public Radio Station (NPR) a piano arrangement of *Gesu Bambino*. It is an Italian Christmas Carol with "O Come, All Ye Faithful" for the chorus. The music was written by Pietro Yon and the lyrics by Frederick Martens.

Suddenly I felt my brother's presence. My brother sang this carol as a solo at a Christmas program when he was ten or eleven years old in the basement of the Baptist church in our hometown, West Point, Virginia. He was taught *Gesu* by the minister's son, Bobby Pleasants, who also was an organist and my piano teacher. I wonder where he is now. I give thanks today for Bobby for the gift he gave me in teaching my brother to sing this ethereal Christmas anthem so many years ago. I see and hear my young brother singing like a cherub in the candlelight, lifting his head and his eyes as he strains for the high notes, singing with all his might.

This was a Christmas gift from my brother. He was physically very strong. I myself have many mobility issues. This Christmas Eve we had two very well-attended services at St. Mark's. I have been concerned whether I could physically serve as one of the deacons at these demanding services late at night which almost a thousand people will attend. That morning before Christmas Eve I was empowered. I felt my brother and his strength beside me. I had no doubt that this was something I could do, and I still feel his strength and love throughout these twelve days of Christmas.

Buechner, Lewis: Telling Secrets on New Year's Eve

"I have come to believe that by and large the human family all has the same secrets, which are both very telling and very important to tell."

—Frederick Buechner in *Telling Secrets* (HarperOne, 1991), p. 2.

In *Telling Secrets,* Buechner reminds us that we so often are like the dwarves in the stable in *The Last Battle* by C. S. Lewis. We do not see the good and do not realize that we are surrounded by beauty, but live trapped lives because of our dark secrets. We are as sick as our secrets and can get well only by airing these secrets, if only in our own hearts. Like the dwarves, we live our lives huddled together in what we think is a cramped, pitch-black stable where there is little room to breathe.

In reality, we are in the midst of an endless green meadow where the sun is shining and the sky is blue. Aslan himself (God) stands there offering freedom; but the dwarves cannot see him and only see each other.

We are our secrets. Our trusting each other enough to share these secrets has much to do with the secret of *what it is like to be connected to the God within us,* as well as honoring our humanness.

This last day of the calendar year is a good time to take inventory of what secrets we may be carrying into the new year that will keep us in the dark and block our deeper understanding of God within us, God in our neighbor, and God transcendent.

The Present, New Year's Day, Eighth Day of Christmas

"What comes next? The answer is: we never know. No matter how smart we are, how carefully we have planned, or how much data we have gathered, we are still only mortals who can never control the future. We live in the now, in the eternally changing series of spaces we call the present. The now is where we shine. In the now we can have an impact, be creative, shape reality, build relationships that can withstand change. What happens tomorrow may always be a surprise, but what happens today can still feel our presence. In fact, we are the artists of the now. We can turn a moment into a memory, a glance into a promise, an idea into a vision that will last forever."

—Bishop Steven Charleston Daily Facebook Page.

I think I became aware of the gift of living in the present moment in the 1980s when I bought Spencer Johnson's eighty-page book, *The Precious Present,* as a Christmas present for my husband and decided to read it first. It is a practical parable of a man living in our fast-paced world, trying to find meaning and peace, opening the most precious of presents. Later I would read two more of Johnson's books: *The One Minute Manager* and *Who Moved My Cheese?* during my self-help period as I was attempting to cope with the demands of a busy pediatric radiology practice. Then I was reminded again of the power of living in the present when I read in C. S. Lewis' *Screwtape Letters* that God meets us only in the present moment. "The Present is the point at which time touches eternity." This is where God lives in our lives. God is not in the past or the future, but here to greet us in the present.

How do we stay in the present moment? Anthony de Mello in his book *Sadhana* teaches us that living in our body and not living only out of our head keeps us grounded. Spending time in nature connects us to the present. Being with children keeps us in the present, for that is where they live.

Living in the "now" can be our gift to ourselves, to God, and to all we will meet in this new year.

Rohr: Low Point, Blue Christmas

"When you have not yet learned what transformation feels or looks like, someone—perhaps some loving human or simply God's own embrace—needs to hold you now because you cannot hold yourself. When we experience this radical holding, and even deep loving, this is salvation!"

—Richard Rohr, adapted from *Great Themes of Paul: Life As Participation* (Franciscan Media, 2002), disc 10.

The holidays are often the hardest time for those who have experienced the death of a loved one. Some congregations hold "Blue Christmas" services to let people in mourning know that the church recognizes their loss.

I have been involved as a facilitator with an eight-week grief recovery group, Walking the Mourner's Path, for more than fifteen years. In it we minister to people who are near their lowest point after the death of child, a spouse, a parent, a brother, a sister, a partner. We do witness despair, especially after tragic deaths such as the death of the young; but perspectives do change. Sometimes there is only a small transformation; sometimes it is huge. By deciding to come to the group, the participants have made a positive commitment to seek transformation; so they have already taken a step forward in a new direction before they come. As facilitators, we are there to bring the group together, to encourage them, to listen to them, to hear them, to give them time to articulate *where they are* in their grief. We are vessels holding the group.

The true healers are the participants themselves. They are the ones who know the most about despair. Individuals are all at different stages of grief. They honor and embrace the each other's place as well. They radically hold and support each other. Some have been participating for a year, others maybe for three months. Mourners know their pain better than anyone else; and they can best share that "road less traveled" toward recovery and resurrection, honoring the lives of those they loved. It is a privilege to be there with them to witness resurrection.

Each year I find myself saying less and less, for the wisdom comes from the group. This is just one more instance of observing *healing in community,* and all we have to do is be present to look for and point out the God in each other.

This week I am having a Christmas and New Year's lunch with a Mourner's Path group that has been meeting annually for more than six years—continuing to support and love each other, especially during the holidays. They have seen Good Friday. They and I go this morning to hear their stories of Incarnation and epiphany and resurrection.

Society of St. John the Evangelist: Offer Companionship on the Tenth Day of Christmas

"As we approach the Christmas season, think of someone in your own life who is sad, or lonely, or hurting, and pledge to say or do something to help bring God's healing love into their lives. Invite them for a coffee, or a meal. Pay them a visit. Phone them. Show them that they are not alone."

—Br. Geoffrey Tristram, SSJE, in "Brother, Give Us a Word," a daily email sent to friends and followers of the Society of Saint John the Evangelist, a religious order for men in the Episcopal/Anglican Church. www.ssje.org

The Brothers of St. John the Evangelist offer us a reminder of gifts we have to offer for Christmas. There are twelve days of Christmas between Christmas Day and the celebration of Epiphany on January 6. These should be slow- down times for us when we can re-center. Many children are still out of school, waiting for us to play with them. There is no better way to connect to the Christ born within us than to connect to the newly born Christ in children. The young have not yet developed any worldly masks of protection which can often hide Christ's essence.

We all have neighbors and friends we have neglected because of our busyness. This is the time to offer to them our precious gift of time. Being present with them takes us to where the Christ child has been born and is waiting to see us as well.

Brueggemann, Benedict: Christians Living in the New Year

"The gift of Christmas contradicts everything we sense about our own life."

—Walter Brueggemann in *Celebrating Abundance: Devotions for Advent* (Westminster John Knox Press, 2017), p. 67.

We listen to the news. We become depressed. Every day something more terrible happens. We feel helpless, powerless. The gift of love, the gift of Christmas does bring hope. I keep thinking about St. Benedict. The world is crashing all around him. Rome is being destroyed by Germanic invaders who have taken over his country. He tries to escape and become a hermit. It doesn't work. He joins a community. He decides the community needs a new way to live together in love and consideration for others, and develops The Rule of Benedict.

This is of course an oversimplification of this part of history.

The beginning of the prologue to The Rule is, "Listen with the ear of your heart." This is the call I hear this Christmas season. We are being called to a more intentional living of the Rule of Benedict in community. I am presently beginning a review of The Rule to present to the Community of Hope and Daughters of the King in the next few weeks. Community of Hope is a Benedictine pastoral care program for non-ordained persons. The Daughters of the King are women in our congregation called to an intentional life of prayer. I give thanks for friends who decided to study Benedictine spirituality in these two programs in the new year. They may think we are helping to train them. Maybe so; but in reality, we are all retraining in both of these programs as we prepare for intentional living in love and prayer in the coming new year.

Rohr: Contemplation and Action

"The dance of action and contemplation is an art form that will take your entire life to master. Like Moses at the burning bush, many of us begin with a mystical moment and end with social action or what looks like politics."

—Richard Rohr in *Dancing Standing Still: Healing the World from a Place of Prayer* (Paulist Press, 2014), pp. 6, 11.

Life indeed is a dance in which we either sit on the sidelines as mystics contemplating the love of God—or bravely go onto the dance floor as activists for those who have been harmed by fear. An ideal life would include doing both; but balance often isn't our strong suit.

When I returned to the life of a "religious" person after a five-year interlude of retreating from spiritual pursuits, I had an insatiable hunger to read and study about God. I think this grew out of my medical training. If doctors want to know about a subject, we research and study in depth what has already been written about it.

Then, for some unknown reason, I began to write about what I was experiencing. Again, the incentive to write may have come from my training in academic medicine spilling into my spiritual life—a compulsion to "publish or perish."

I remember on one December night reading an Advent piece at an early Christmas gathering of the women of St. Mark's. Mrs. Metcalf, a renowned speech teacher who also sat on our pew at the church, said to me in passing as we were going to pick up our plates for dinner, "It is good to see another mystic."

Mystic. I never thought of myself as a mystic; but suddenly I knew I had just been anointed one by a master. Again, I think medical training was a proving ground for me to develop some insight into God's presence at work in the world. My job as a radiologist is to look for the unknown, finding evidence in the shadows and often in the dark through the imaging techniques of X-rays or ultrasounds. Radiologists examine an inside, hidden world that is just beneath the surface.

God uses every aspect of our personal experience. No skill or insight is wasted. Eventually, over many, many years of just writing about spiritual experience, I have been moved to action: making phone calls, writing letters, marching, visiting the sick and dying, aiding those who have difficulty getting groceries, advocating for prisoners and immigrants, supporting homeless veterans, working with people in recovery. As long as we can see the love of God in our contemplation *and* in our action, we will know one of the fruits of the spirit: peace. When one peace or "piece" is missing, I know I am off track.

I share this dance during the last day of the Christmas season, and look forward to learning from the mystic part of each of us—that also is seeking to recognize how God will appear next on our dance card in this new year.

EPIPHANY

Meeting Epiphany

"Arise, shine; for your light has come,
and the glory of the Lord has risen upon you."

—Isaiah 60:1.

On Sunday we are celebrating the Feast Day of Epiphany, the manifestation of the light of Christ to the Gentiles. That's most of us. I first met Epiphany when I was eleven or maybe twelve years old. A boyfriend and his parents took me to visit "her" on the icy winter night of January 6 in the mid-1950s. I sat in the candlelight glow of the small Episcopal church in my hometown in tidewater Virginia, and heard her ancient liturgy and her haunting mystic melodies. As we walked out of the small-town white wooden church into the bitter cold January night carrying our small candles, the first winter's snow also came down to celebrate her. Epiphany led me to an experience I wanted to relive again and again.

Epiphany revealed to me a living presence, a God greater than myself—who was also greater than time, immanent and transcendent.

But as often happens with such early experiences, I soon became immersed in growing up and going to school and succeeding in life—and I let her slip away. I did not again seek her out for many years—in fact, until I was a junior in medical school. I was studying and working at a frantic pace. My marriage had recently failed. I felt alone, exhausted, and damaged. I was open to Epiphany's call. I contacted the Dean of the Episcopal Cathedral in Memphis, William Dimmick, and he led me by the hand back to her feast day, this time in St. Mary's Cathedral.

On that Sunday closest to January 6, the darkened stone church was packed with young people. On this occasion I heard haunting, ancient chant as well as contemporary music. The priest of the Greek Orthodox Church read the Gospel in Greek. At this service three ornately adorned Wise Men sang as they slowly and majestically processed down the long center aisle of the nave and laid their gifts on the memorial altar. The service ended as we sang hymns, and the cathedral came ablaze as our candles were lighted. We continued to sing with the Wise Men as we moved now in the opposite direction, recessing from the altar and venturing into the dark night—taking our new light out into the world beyond the cathedral.

Since that January 6th I have stayed with Epiphany, and she has been my companion now for fifty years. Each year we continue to celebrate her gifts for the twelve days following the feast of Christmas Day. She is a reminder of God's coming, God's presence revealed to the entire world, not just to a chosen few. We are strengthened by worshiping, in new and old ways, the manifestation of the living, immanent, incarnate God. And as we are strengthened and enlightened by her, we are called to take her light, love, and enlightenment out—out into a world that is often cold and exhausted, dark and damaged and lonely.

Epiphany yearly also brings us one more revelation. Out in the world, we see her path in the dark night more clearly because of her great light from so many shining candles beyond our own.

May this new year be full of many more epiphanies for all of us and for those we love.

Charleston: Magdalene, The World Within

"How hard it is sometimes to live in two worlds, the one we inhabit with the people around us, and the one that we live in alone. None may know the pain we hide, the deep wells of worry into which we look, the memories that enfold our lives like a forest. But the Spirit knows and cares and understands, ever beside us to offer comfort and counsel."

—Bishop Steven Charleston Daily Facebook Page.

The Repentant Magdalene.

Recently I spent time with a 387-year-old friend that I have known for her last twenty-five years. We first met when she was one of three Georges de La Tour's Magdalene paintings at a special exhibition at the National Gallery of Art. She was the only one in their permanent collection. I visited her that morning before an important meeting in Washington, and she quieted my soul. I instantly fell in love with her. She spoke to me as no other painting has before or since. This Magdalene sits with her left hand on a skull. She does not look at the skull directly but sees the skull's image in a mirror in front of her. The chiaroscuro scene is dark and only illumined by a partially hidden candle beside the skull. I talk to Magdalene and thank her for her insights.

For me, the skull represents our insides, what our skin covers up—the Christ within as well as the negative parts of our unconscious. Over the years this Magdalene has taught me that we most often see inside ourselves by looking into a reflection, a mirror. It is too painful and too overwhelming to see what we are beneath our surface. We cannot look there directly. It is like looking at the sun. The mirror represents the reflection we see of ourselves in others. We come to know and understand the true parts of ourselves by seeing ourselves in our neighbors.

One of the reasons God calls us to community is to learn from others who we really are. I best see my own soul, the Christ within me, as well as my many unconscious character defects, by first recognizing them in others. Caring for our life means discovering these unconscious character defects first by becoming aware, and then by seeing them for what they are in others. Caring for our soul is finding the Christ within ourselves by first seeing that holy in another, and then realizing the miracle that it is also within us.

May we continue to experience these epiphanies around us, especially through art and culture.

Thich Nhat Hanh: Walking Meditation

"People say that walking on water is a miracle, but to me, walking peacefully on the earth is the real miracle."

—Thich Nhat Hanh in *The Long Road Turns to Joy: A Guide to Walking Meditation* (Parallax Press, 1996), p. 58.

For many years, I would walk around the block in my neighborhood for twenty minutes before going to work at the hospital. This seems to quiet the "committee meeting" in my head. Putting my feet on the earth, even the pavement of the road, seems to reconnect my head to my body as I become "grounded." Always when I am outside, I realize there is a world greater than the one I live in. There is a power greater than myself. I have trouble meditating when I am simply sitting; but any movement such as walking can lead me into that meditative journey.

The Vietnamese Buddhist, Thich Nhat Hanh, is one of the most well known meditative walkers. His pocket-sized book is full of simple mindfulness exercises to practice as we walk. He introduces us to several methods of gauging and listening to our breath as we walk. He teaches us to be aware of the ground, and of our foot as it touches the ground, as well as of our breath. I established the pattern of breathing in on the drop of the right foot, out out on the drop of the left. This was similar to walking the labyrinth and paying close attention to the path.

In mindful walking, as we stay with our breath, we find there are no more rooms available for that committee to meet in our heads. Thich Nhat Hanh compares walking to eating, nourishing our bodies with each step. As we walk, we massage the earth. When the baby Buddha was born, he was said to have taken seven steps, and that a Lotus flower blossomed under each step. Thich Nhat Hanh suggests we imagine, with each of our steps, a flower blossoming.

We can practice mindful walking anywhere—between meetings, in hospitals, at airports, walking to our car. The Buddhist monk also offers several poems to recite while walking: "I have arrived, I am home, in the here, in the now. I am solid. I am free. In the ultimate I dwell."

St. Francis: Hoeing; Gandhi: Dying

"Saint Francis, hoeing his garden, was asked what he would do if he knew the world would end tomorrow. 'Continue hoeing my garden,' said the saint."

—Suzanne Guthrie.

I have often heard this phrase attributed to St. Francis, and wondered what I would do if I knew I was about to die. I have made writing every day a discipline for almost two years—one of my best spiritual practices. Would I keep on writing? As I look outside to trees and birds and sky from the floor-to-ceiling window in my office, and my fingers hit the keyboard, I feel a peace that I hope is God's presence.

I know I would spend as much of the last day with my family—actually, as much as possible. I might entice my grandchildren to watch a movie with me and then just secretly watch them. I would want to be with my husband as much as possible. By actions and words, I would want to make certain my family and friends knew how much I loved them. I would like to have a meal with my family and friends. I would look at old pictures to keep memories with me. I would spend more time with the family pictures and icons and remembrances of joy that surround my desk. I would ask for prayers from the good pray-ers I know, especially the women in Daughters of the King. I would also spend time in prayer at a sacred space.

Of course, if everyone else knew the world was coming to an end, it would be interesting to see how our paths might cross!

So, what does all this mean?

"Live as if you were to die tomorrow. Learn as if you were to live forever," is attributed to Mahatma Gandhi.

I try to carry these two quotes by Gandhi and St. Francis with me each day and share them with spiritual friends as well. The quotes are a good daily benchmark as to whether we are doing the practices that bring us closer to God.

Gandhi's quote is a paradox, an anchor metaphor for our life, which is a constant ambiguous paradox. Each day this year I hope to spend more of my time doing things to help me realize my best connections to God, as well as to myself, my neighbors, my family, and my friends.

Of course, often the connections lead me to other places, and I pray to stay open to these new adventures.

Blessing

"The Lord spoke to Moses, saying: Speak to Aaron and his sons, saying, Thus you shall bless the Israelites: You shall say to them,
The Lord bless you and keep you;
the Lord make his face to shine upon you, and be gracious to you;
the Lord lift up his countenance upon you, and give you peace.
So they shall put my name on the Israelites, and I will bless them."

—Numbers 6:22-27.

This passage from Numbers is used frequently as a benediction in so many congregations. This morning, for some reason, I stop and really listen to the words. We are giving God human characteristics. Attributing human reactions and feelings to God, as you know, falls under a big word with rolling syllables: *anthropomorphism*. Sometimes this is our only way to express what we would like to say about God. It has its traps; but it can on occasion give us the tiniest glimpses of the magnitude of the love and care we receive from God.

How wonderful to pray that "God's face" will be directed to us—and even more that God's face will *shine* on us, and we will receive God's grace. We are asking God to look directly at us—look us right in the eye and give us peace. We are indeed asking for a connection, a blessing—an ancient blessing that was bestowed on the Hebrews and now comes down to us many centuries later.

I love knowing that the early Hebrews were just people like us, asking for a blessing, a relationship; calling on God to look directly at them and to bring them peace.

What is the face of God? Is it the horizon, the stars, the oceans, the forests, the moon, all of space as far as we can see? Is it the Solar System, the planets Mars and Jupiter—or is it a multitude of solar systems and beyond? We have come full circle back to the word *solar*—which pertains to the sun, with a brightness that shines for us above all other bodies. Yet we know that the brightness of our sun pales in the face of *the love of our God* that shines on sunny as well as dark days and nights.

Outrageous

"We have lost, I think, our proper sense of outrage, and what God does is often outrageous for no matter how much we think we know how God will act, God frequently acts in other incomprehensible and outrageous ways."

—Br. James Koester, SSJE, in "Brother, Give Us a Word," a daily email sent to friends and followers of the Society of Saint John the Evangelist, a religious order for men in the Episcopal/Anglican Church. www.ssje.org

What is outrageous? Every sunrise and each sunset. The flowers and flowering plants and bushes and trees that appear in sequence in spring; the crocuses, camellias, redbuds, forsythia, daffodils, tulips, Bradford Pear trees, climbing wisteria, azaleas, roses, lilies, irises, magnolias, hydrangeas, geraniums, and finally the crape myrtle that last through the summer. Is there more? What about the yellow and red and orange autumn leaves on a crisp fall day? How about the secret waterfall that only you and a few friends and family know of? What about floating in the Buffalo River? Or the view from Petit Jean Mountain or Mount Magazine? What about Two Rivers Trail along the Arkansas River?

I am just listing wonders that occupy a small part of Arkansas; but I know each of you has many more outrageous spectacles to share.

I don't know about you, but "outrageous" meets me at every turn. When we look for her, we have only words of gratitude. Outrageous describes our family members and friends who still love us even after getting to know us better. Even more outrageous is the unconditional love of God. This is love that God gives us in more ways than we can understand—knowledge too deep for words. As we try to stay connected to God and listen, we get little outrageous nudges, "not right; yes, this is right." Whenever I go against those gut feelings, I end up in a bad place.

I look back on my life and see how cared for I have been, even when I went down wrong paths. This is outrageous. This is the off-the-scale love of God: to stick with us in our habit of taking one step forward, two steps back. We cannot comprehend such love. We can only try in our feeble way to observe it and remember it and give thanks for the outrageous love and beauty given us.

Mosaic Community

"When I am with a group of human beings committed to hanging in there through both the agony and the joy of community, I have a dim sense that I am participating in a phenomenon for which there is only one word ... glory."

—M. Scott Peck.

This morning I think of groups I am in, especially a Wednesday morning book group which has met for more years than I can remember. We started in one church as an Education for Ministry or EfM group, and later morphed into a Disciples of Christ in Community or DOCC Transforming the Literature of the Bible study group. We moved to other churches as the bishop reassigned me, and each time collected different members. We continued to read contemporary literature and Scripture, and looked for patterns to follow in the lives of those who share our Judeo-Christian heritage. Very few members now attend the same congregation, and we are always enriched by people of other faith groups. We are now back meeting at our home, next to our fireplace in the den. My husband always puts fresh flowers on the coffee table. There is something about being in a home, as well as meeting with an eclectic group of people who have learned to accept each other deeply and lovingly—so that our discussions can easily ignite into "God moments."

Another amazing image of such a community is a mosaic of pieces of cut glass of different shapes and colors. Each individual may be beautiful in his or her own right; but when we are together, a truly glorious multicolored image emerges.

I think of the story that I often tell children, given to me so many years ago by Dean McMillin, another spiritual friend. God wanted to give part of God to God's creation. So God took a huge mirror, looked into it, and broke the mirror into many tiny pieces, sending them down to earth. God gave to every one of us a tiny piece, a reflection of God. We spend years trying to find that piece of God within ourselves; and when we do, we get so excited, we cry, "I have found God."

That is where the journey stops for so many, who try to prioritize *their* piece, *their* image of God, as the only one that is truly of God. But God calls us to another task. We are to fit our piece in with those of all others. As we fit together more and more pieces of God that we have found in others, our image of God becomes deeper and fuller.

We sometimes meet people whose image of God is so foreign to us, so different from ours. Sometimes these people are even our children! As we piece together more and more facets and see so many other parts that represent God, we come closer to their part—perhaps on the edge of our own God image.

This is a journey of a lifetime: finding God in ourselves, connecting it to the God in others, and enlarging our image of God. A beautiful mosaic. It is called community.

Baptism

"This dying and rising, this crossing over from death to life which happens at baptism, is not a one-off thing—but it is to be our daily vesture as Christians."

—Br. Geoffrey Tristram, SSJE, in "Brother, Give Us a Word," a daily email sent to friends and followers of the Society of Saint John the Evangelist, a religious order for men in the Episcopal/Anglican Church. www.ssje.org

If we were baptized in a river or by full immersion, we might better understand this well-known theological concept of Baptism as a dying and rebirth, and compare it to our life in the world. There is something appropriate about going totally under water in the arms of someone else, totally surrendering—and wondering for a brief second if we will resurface. When we do again experience our heads above water, we cannot help but look around, shake our head of dripping hair, and give thanks for being alive—a new beginning, a fresh start, a new person. Suddenly we see the world a little clearer. Some of the fog is gone.

Each day a little of us certainly dies physically. Each day we try to learn a little more about surrender. My prayer is that each day a few of my character defects die or are chipped away. When that happens, I do indeed know resurrection, a new life, a life of peace and love and joy. But as so often happens, pieces of those character defects or sins seem to come right back, like magnets, to places in our mind and body and spirit where they once so comfortably lived. Sometimes they return like some fiery, ugly dragon from a place inside of us that we never knew existed, and we end up having to make more apologies than we did in the past.

Baptism in our tradition is a onetime thing; but dying and resurrection are a daily, sometimes hourly event. The concept that in Baptism we experience dying and resurrection is still important. I love Br. Geoffrey's use of the word *vesture,* meaning a garment that covers us like a vestment. He is offering to us the opportunity to try to imagine *wearing our baptism* like a vestment throughout the day. An amazing concept!

As we watch infants, toddlers, youth, and adults being baptized, we might imagine them putting on vestments to cover them throughout eternal life, as a sign that they are marked as God's own forever. God is always with them in each dying and each resurrection in their lives. We hold on to this sacrament as an outward and visible sign and symbol of our life, in and with Christ in the world.

There are parts of us that are dying, but there are parts of us that *need* to die; and God offers resurrection to us daily at each death on both sides of the veil.

The Clark Fork River and Love

"And so it is those we live with and should know who elude us, but we can still love them. We can love completely without complete understanding."

—Norman Maclean in *A River Runs Through It* (University of Chicago Press, 1976).

This past summer we were in Missoula, Montana, visiting our daughter Joanna and her husband Dennis, along with our oldest grandson, Mac, and his dad John. Our hotel is right, I mean *directly* on the banks of Clark Fork, and the river actually is, rapidly, in real time, running by our small porch on the first floor. We are mesmerized by watching the high-speed water; but it is the sound of the racing river that truly runs through us. It calms. It soothes. In its orchestral movement, it is peaceful. It sounds like a wind instrument, perhaps a distant Native American flute. Sometimes it has the *"Om"* sound that is chanted in yoga and Eastern meditation. We begin to know the stillness of sitting or standing and just observing the wonder—watching something go by that is too magnificent for words. Gazing at it, we can become so relaxed that we fall asleep. Water, moving or still, has healing powers that we cannot understand.

Today we hear from our daughter that all of this is covered with snow; but I know that the sound of the Clark Fork is still mesmerizing lives.

I have watched the Robert Redford movie, *A River Runs Through It,* with all of our children and most of our grandchildren. We can often quote lines from the movie and return the responding lines to each other. If you have not read the book or seen the movie, stop now—because I am going to spoil it for you.

The story is about the Maclean family, a father and two sons, Norman and Paul, growing up and fly-fishing in Missoula, Montana. The words quoted above come near the end of the movie, included in one of the father's last sermons. I could almost hear Norman's father when we rode by that same brick Presbyterian church last summer on the way to get ice cream. The father is indirectly talking about Norman's younger brother, Paul, who died an early traumatic death related to his addictions.

As I watch and listen beside the Clark Fork, where the Macleans lived and loved a century ago, I think also of those people I could not understand but wanted to love completely. My prayers today are to keep trying to hear these words by Norman's father as they apply to them. Of course, there are also those I could not understand and never even wanted to consider loving the least bit, much less completely. I pray a little more to see those people in a new light.

Loving without understanding may be a stage on the path to unconditional love, God's love. *Om.*

Benedictine Life

"Listen carefully, my child to my instructions, and attend to them with the ear of your heart."

—Prologue to The Rule of Benedict.

Benedict of Nursia in the 6th century tried to follow a spiritual path by himself and realized he instead needed to practice this in community. From his awareness, we now have The Rule of Benedict, a way to find and follow God in community—balancing work, study, sleep, worship and prayers, and recreation. This Rule has now been used for centuries in Benedictine monasteries. Today people are developing ways to follow a rule as they live in the secular world, still connecting in community with spiritual friends and spiritual directors.

This Prologue to The Rule is my favorite part of the treatise: "Listen with the ear of your heart." This is the call to the spiritual life, a way to live in the world still connected to God. First, we are to listen, to pay attention. We are called to awaken the ear of our heart. Through this we learn to connect to something outside of ourselves, hearing and loving. We hear and listen and learn about love most evidently in community, finding our source and inspiration in the other.

There are many outstanding books about The Rule of Benedict. I will share three favorites, but would like to hear about books that have been most helpful as *you* try to find your rule of life. The Rule of Benedict: A Spirituality for the 21st Century, by Joan Chittister, is used by The International Community of Hope, a training program for lay pastoral care ministers that also immerses them in Benedictine spirituality. Joan Chittister writes a short meditation after each part of The Rule and applies it to our everyday life.

Always We Begin Again: The Benedictine Way of Living, by Memphis lawyer John McQuiston II, is a pocket-sized book that can be carried around during the day. It is a modernization of Benedict's Rule with a sample rule of life.

St. Benedict's Toolbox is exactly what the author, Jane Tomaine, calls it in her subtitle: *The Nuts and Bolts of Everyday Benedictine Living.*

All three books are especially good to read together in community, while learning and supporting each other.

The Daughters of the King at my previous church, and now at St. Mark's, are reading *St. Benedict's Toolbox* together. Episcopal priest Dennis Campbell, my daughter's husband, reminds me that *The Book of Common Prayer* is also steeped in Benedictine spirituality!

MLK: Racism, Inconvenient Time

"I have almost reached the regrettable conclusion that the Negro's great stumbling block in the stride toward freedom is not the White Citizen's Councillor or the Ku Klux Klanner, but the white moderate who is more devoted to 'order' than to justice; who prefers a negative peace which is the absence of tension to a positive peace which is the presence of justice.."

—Martin Luther King, Jr., "Letter from Birmingham Jail," April 16, 1963.

I receive a letter from a friend encouraging me that I am in a position to speak out against racism. I am at a dream retreat and the presenter, also my spiritual director, tells the story several times about Jacob's dream of a heavenly ladder. Jacob renames the place of his dream Bethel, *house of God, God is present*. I suddenly think of Bethel AME Church in Little Rock, where I fell in love with that African American congregation as they taught us all about racism and poverty. I had been assigned to Trinity Cathedral in Little Rock, and we planned together a celebration of the anniversary of the 1957 desegregation of Central High School. Later our daughter went there, and now a granddaughter is attending that historic school. In the past I have gone to a prayer breakfast at our sister St. Mark Baptist Church for the celebration of King's birthday on January 15. Being there was empowering.

This week people all over the world will be celebrating the life of Martin Luther King, Jr., who died more than fifty years ago on April 4,

1968. I feel some ownership in his death since I was a senior medical student in Memphis when he was assassinated. At that time, my world centered solely on finishing medical school. His death made it more difficult for me to get to the hospital, since Memphis was briefly under a curfew and martial law. I do remember what the Dean of St. Mary's Cathedral did. He carried the processional cross from the Cathedral and marched with other clergy to Memphis Mayor Loeb's office, petitioning him to bring to an end the injustices that had brought King to Memphis. I also remember that Dean Dimmick's speaking out with his feet brought consequences for him at the Cathedral, as he lost a large part of his congregation.

So here we are, more than fifty years later. How are we to carry the cross with our hands, as so many before us have modeled for us—walking out into the streets and going to the homes and schools and hospitals of our cities and countrysides, speaking and acting the truth with love against the violence and hatred that still lives?

I know I am a storyteller. I share my story with you; but especially today I offer it to my children and grandchildren, surrounding them with love and prayers that they may be empowered to do a better job than we did.

MLK: A New Norm of Greatness

"Jesus gave us a new norm of greatness. You don't have to have a college degree to serve. You don't have to make your subject and your verb agree to serve. You don't have to know about Plato and Aristotle to serve. You don't have to know the second theory of thermodynamics in physics to serve. You only need a heart full of grace, a soul generated by love."

—Martin Luther King, Jr., in his sermon "Drum Major Instinct," Atlanta, Georgia, February 4, 1968.

Here Martin Luther King is giving us the short version of servant ministry, which Bishop Bennett Sims wrote about in 1997 in his landmark book, Servanthood: Leadership for the Third Millennium. Our worthiness has nothing to do with our I. Q. Being a servant leader is completely different from being the smartest; working to become the greatest; needing to control; or seeking the admiration of others because of one's abilities. Servant leaders make room for and empower others. They work to build up others, not to polish the system or pump up the leader's self-importance. A servant leader does not see productivity or results as the prime purpose of any family system, endeavor, church, or business. Human enhancement, not human employment, is the primary aim of organizations led by servant leaders. Meaning and joy in work come from power with, not power over. Sims describes collaboration with others as the "meat and potatoes" of human nourishment; while competition is the "salt and pepper." He believes our society has been living on "spices."

Grace, Flat Tire

"We are very imperfect vehicles for the embodiment of Divine Grace. We're all driving around on at least one flat tire and with missing or malfunctioning parts. Broken as we are, the impulse is still there: Christ's desire to incarnate grace and truth."

—Br. Mark Brown, SSJE, in "Brother, Give Us a Word," a daily email sent to friends and followers of the Society of Saint John the Evangelist, a religious order for men in the Episcopal/Anglican Church. www.ssje.org

I and another spiritual friend so relate to this message, as we both have mobility issues. That is why we love the image that we are *moving around with at least one flat tire*—and maybe more. Images from our physical life are mirrors into our spiritual life. These images help us know a God who is all knowing, and of whom we receive only a tiny glimpse from time to time.

I hope to remember the flat tire when I make my mistakes. It helps me to acknowledge that I am human and not beat myself up. I just need a little more air, a little more Spirit in my tires. I like the image of the Spirit being the air we breathe. It is also the freely given breath of creation, the mark of the Creator, that is all around us.

Sometimes our tires become so worn that we actually will have to change them. That could mean so many things. The Spirit can no longer be confined within our tires. Maybe we are ready to begin a new spiritual practice. Or it is a sign that our image of God has become too small. Perhaps it means old habits will no longer work to keep us connected.

The flat tire is a work in progress. It is a reminder that we are not perfection and are subject to change.

De Mello: Selfish

"Part of waking up is that you live your life as you see fit. And understand: That is not selfish. The selfish thing is to demand that someone else live their life as YOU see fit."

—Anthony de Mello.

Anthony de Mello was an Indian Jesuit priest and psychotherapist who died too young in 1987, but whose spiritual writings still speak clearly to us today. I think de Mello is trying to tell us that loving others means supporting them and allowing them to be the person God created them to be. Self-love or selfishness consists in wanting others to be the person *we* want them to be. This is a constant struggle because "we are so wise and have such good ideas!" Sometimes we want others to live a certain way, to live out a life along a path that we ourselves were not able to live. Other times it is a control issue, assuming we know what is best for someone else.

We struggle with this form of selfishness with our children, our grandchildren, our students, our partners, our friends—in almost any relationship. Of course, this also can be a hurdle to overcome in spiritual direction: wanting our spiritual friends to live out a certain form of spirituality, especially a pattern of spiritual living that has worked for us.

Spiritual direction is a two-way street. It is like teaching or any form of mentoring. If we are not learning from our spiritual friends as well as sharing with them, we become even more self-absorbed in our own knowledge and experience. We must constantly remember that we look to *the Holy Spirit* to be present with us in spiritual direction, guiding and teaching us and our spiritual friends.

My experience is that two things are helpful. First, trying to live the Serenity Prayer, knowing we can change only ourselves and not others. God is the one who effects change. We are to sit back and wait for the Holy Spirit to bring about transformation.

The second is awareness: awareness of at what point we think we know what is best for others and start planning their agenda—not allowing them to become the person the Christ, the Spirit within, is leading them to be. I am counting on the Holy Spirit to bring in de Mello holding up a big stop sign with SELFISH written all over it whenever I become aware that I am doing this!

Next, we are to turn around and prayerfully and humbly ask God to transform that selfish energy directed at others into *energy for the Christ within us* to continue creating us as the person God birthed us to be.

Hibbs: Jesus Prayer

"Lord Jesus Christ, Son of God, have mercy on me, a sinner."

Last summer we were at Camp Allen in Texas for the first time at a Community of Hope International conference at which Mary Earle was the keynote speaker. As I look over her books, I find this newly published 20th anniversary edition of *An Altar in Your Heart: Meditations on the Jesus Prayer,* by Bishop Robert Hibbs, with a Foreword by Mary Earle. The Jesus Prayer has been my mantra in the early morning and at evening as I go to sleep. I pray the prayer during any time of anxiety or fear or temptation during the day or night, especially during medical tests for myself and my family. It is my feeble attempt at praying without ceasing.

I have known Bishop Hibbs for years through work with the Episcopal Recovery Community, but I never knew about his work on the Jesus Prayer. As I share with Mary my connection to Bishop Hibbs, I find out he died a year ago in April, and that Mary preached the homily at his funeral service. I want to thank and honor him for the support he gave me and so many others in recovery by sharing this book with you. Also included is an audio CD of his lectures at a retreat that produced the book, which the Cajuns would call a *lagniappe,* a little something extra. For years Bob Hibbs was the major voice for recovery in the Episcopal House of Bishops.

Saying the Jesus Prayer is like using a prayer rope or beads, but in our heads. Bishop Hibbs relates the story of Hungarian Cardinal Mindszenty and Father Eschmann, who survived torture and solitary imprisonment by staying connected to God through the Jesus Prayer.

The first words of the Jesus Prayer, "Lord Jesus Christ, Son of God," remind us of both Jesus' *divinity* and his *humanity,* which Hibbs believes is an important constant affirmation to keep us in relationship with Jesus. These first words of the prayer with Jesus' name express Easter, the *Alleluia* part of the prayer. The last phrase about mercy expresses Good Friday. Sister Carol Perry at this same conference reminds us that in this request we are making the choice to ask for *God's mercy in our lives,* rather than God's justice based on how we have lived our lives. Hibbs believes we continually live in the tension between rejoicing in Easter and remaining connected to Good Friday.

Bishop Hibbs reminds us that this is an oral prayer to be said out loud as much as possible, especially as we begin to make the Jesus Prayer a part of our being. He cautions us not to be discouraged as we become distracted while we say it. We are gently to return to the prayer without judgment on ourselves. We are to deal with distractions in a manner similar to the way we treat the ones we encounter in Centering Prayer. We might see them as barges moving down the Mississippi or any favorite river. We are to let them pass on by without interacting with them.

Eventually the prayer develops a rhythm in our lives and becomes a gift from God, closely related to the beating of our heart—a constant, habitual recollection or awareness of God's presence. Hibbs also reminds us that when we pray the Jesus Prayer, we are attempting to connect to Jesus, God, the Spirit—the Trinity above and beyond us—but also to the Christ in our neighbor and in ourselves.

For people in 12-step recovery, this is where the steps intersect with the Jesus Prayer, as we "sought through prayer and meditation to improve our conscious contact with God" (Step 11, Chapter 5, "How It Works," *The Big Book of Alcoholics Anonymous,* 2016), p. 85.

Sometimes I modify the prayer to be similar to what is called Agnus Dei, the fraction anthem said or sung after breaking the bread in the Eucharist: "Lord God, Lamb of God, that takest away the sins of the world, have mercy on me."

When we meet with someone for spiritual direction or with spiritual friends, we give them our utmost attention; but if we also have the Jesus Prayer running through our mind and heart, we can continue to stay connected to the Spirit who is speaking to the Christ in both of us.

What Langley Knows

"Call to me and I will answer you and tell you great and unsearchable things you do not know."

—Jeremiah 33:3.

This past weekend at our oldest granddaughter's high school graduation, a Scripture verse was read as each graduate walked across the stage to receive his or her diploma. The verse had been chosen by the student's high school advisor. The above verse was read as Langley received her diploma. What an amazing promise to hold onto for the rest of her life.

We only need to call to God, and God will answer. God will tell us unimaginable things that we need to know. Calling on God can mean praying for God's presence; but it also can mean sitting in silence and *waiting* for God's presence inside and outside of us to become manifested. It can mean being open to seeing God, Christ, in others. It can mean experiencing God in all of creation and learning how to protect it and care for it. It can mean being open to receiving the love of Christ from another. I have mentioned only a few of the many ways that God asks us to make that call.

The second part, the answer, comes to us through so many different avenues as well. If we expect to hear a voice or receive a sign a few minutes after we make our dial-up to God, we may be disappointed. Direct access and connections to God are beyond our comprehension. Yet answers can come at the most unexpected times, and often are presented to us by the least likely people. At times answers are given by those we barely know, and we can get them even from people we consider our adversaries. Sometimes our bodies provide us with an answer, showing us that we have more or less energy for a calling. Sometimes the answers come to us years later. Our only job is to be open and receptive to God's answers.

How will we know God's answer? Jeremiah tells us we will receive knowledge we never expected to acquire. The 12-step promises can be helpful: "We will know a new freedom and a new happiness. We will intuitively know how to handle situations which used to baffle us. We will suddenly realize that God is doing for us what we could not do for ourselves." —*The Big Book of Alcoholic Anonymous,* pp. 83-84.

Feeling and knowing the fruit of the Spirit in Galatians 5:22-23 is another means of realizing we have received an answer. We become aware that we are living in "love, joy, peace, forbearance, kindness, faithfulness, gentleness, and self-control."

I know I am not telling Langley anything she does not already know.

This verse indeed was already written on her heart.

Merton: Prayer as Distraction

"If my prayer is centered in myself, if it seeks only an enrichment of my own self, my prayer itself will be my greatest potential distraction."

—Thomas Merton in *Thoughts in Solitude* (Farrar, Straus and Giroux, 1999).

Thomas Merton reminds us what our prayer life, and the rest of our life as well, becomes when it is centered on ourselves, our own desires, our own needs, our own knowledge. Merton calls this kind of life a distraction— something that keeps us from the truth; a diversion, a disturbance of the mind; a hindrance. We think we are doing everything right; but in essence we are back where we started, with our world centered on ourselves rather than on God.

We may think that God is our co-pilot, but we ourselves are acting as pilot. We have such good ideas. God is there to make certain that our ideas, our prayers, are answered. I only have to think about all the outcomes that I prayed for that were not answered, that I later learned would have been disastrous—such as the boyfriends who never gave me the time of day and for whom I would have sold my soul. I also well remember the prayers that were answered that became harmful— the jobs I thought I had to have, the co-workers I just knew would be perfect.

As friends in recovery say, "Our best thinking got us here."

When we do not say to God, "Thy will be done," it seems God's answer to us may sometimes be, *"Your* will be done."

Merton is calling us to the prayer of surrender, turning our prayers as well as our life and our wills over to God. *"Thy will be done."*

This kind of prayer and prayer life also calls for acceptance, forgiveness, gratitude, and most of all love—knowing that we are loved beyond any love we could imagine. And that love is daily offered to us, if we only choose to connect to it and accept it.

Kidd: Spiritual Whittling

"Transformation happens not by rejecting these parts of ourselves but by gathering them up and integrating them. Through this process we reach a new wholeness. Spiritual whittling is an encounter with Mystery, waiting, the silence of inner places—all those things most folks no longer have time for."

—Sue Monk Kidd in *When the Heart Waits* (HarperSanFrancisco, 1992).

This is my experience of transformation as well. I constantly realize that once-useful parts of my life that have kept me "together," or kept me connected to God, may be tired and worn and need to rest. These gifts are still a part of me; but what I have to offer has shifted, and my ministry changes. One of the hardest shifts for me was giving up my medical practice that had been my identity; but I was learning that there were so many other things I wanted to do, and it became more and more difficult to keep up with the constantly changing technical medical world.

I also came to learn that just because we are good at one ministry doesn't mean we should keep doing it. We may be preventing others from taking on the joy of that ministry—and actually, they may be able to do it better! What we learn in one part of our life also can be helpful in another ministry, so we need not discard it. In medicine I learned a great deal about suffering, especially about the suffering of children and their parents. I learned how to look deep inside for hidden clues as to what is causing a disease or difficulty. This ability is now helpful in spiritual direction. I also discovered how to work with many varied people. This has helped me to be a little less judgmental and perhaps appreciate personality differences.

I am slowly learning to reevaluate habits that kept me safe during some parts of my life—habits that have later become destructive.

What am I trying to say?

Life is about constantly relinquishing control or the *illusion* that we are in control. It is also about being open to change, letting doors shut—but being open to entering new doors; or not being afraid to sit in the hallway for awhile, waiting to hear the squeak of a new door opening. It is about trusting, avoiding being stuck and stagnating, or thinking we are out of options.

Bolz-Weber: Spiritual vs. Religious

"Spiritual feels individual and escapist. But to be religious (despite all the negative associations with that word) is to be human in the midst of other humans who are as equally messed up and obnoxious and forgiven as ourselves."

—Nadia Bolz-Weber in *Accidental Saints* (Convergent Books, 2016).

Again, and again, Nadia Bolz-Weber makes us sit up and take notice. I have heard so often that phrase, "spiritual but not religious," and I know I have used it as well, and have seen it as a badge of courage. What I hear in it is that a person has a relationship with God, but not with a religious institution or church or creed or denomination. Such a person is trying to "home school" God, as I have actually heard some say. "Spiritual but not religious" people often have been misunderstood or harmed by the institutional church—or they themselves may actually misunderstand the church. I hear this often from people whose perception of church was not *a group of believers in a loving God.* Instead, they were resisting belief in a vengeful God watching their every step in order to catch them doing something wrong. They have been wounded, but some of them do want to have a relationship with God. They are truly seekers.

Bolz-Weber, however, is reminding us that God most often does not call us only to a one- on-one relationship. God also constantly calls us to community—and that is where we will so often experience God in the unlikely humans with whom we learn to live and work.

Charleston: Sacred Within

"Do not be shy about claiming the visions you have seen. I know that in our time and culture it is not as common for people to speak of their spiritual visions, but that does not mean the visions themselves have ceased to appear. The Spirit still sends messages to each of us, images that are unique to our experience, flashes of meaning for us to interpret and understand. Some we seek, some come unbidden, but all are authentic parts of a spiritual life. The sacred is a visual realm. Wisdom is in what we see."

—Bishop Steven Charleston, Daily Facebook Page.

I remember passing by the town of St. Ignatius in the Flathead Indian Reservation on the way to Glacier National Park. The name of Ignatius is sacred to so many of us for what this saint has taught us.

I had previously visited the church there at the foot of the Mission Mountains, which is well known for its original biblical paintings on the ceiling and walls painted by one of the brothers, believed also to be the cook! My daughter tells me that there also had been a school there at which the students were punished if they were caught speaking in their native Salish language. The Jesuits were so certain they were doing the right thing by trying to change the Native Americans into Europeans.

This is a constant reminder for me that we as well sometimes can be so assured about the God of our understanding, and what we have to share, that we forget to honor that part of God in our neighbor whom we are trying to help. Our hope is that we will first always honor the God of the understanding of our spiritual friends. We may tell them about the God of love we know, and share our experience; but we do not insist that this is the *only* way to encounter God.

Each of us has a part of the divine within. Our job is to realize that part of God within us and help those we meet to find the God within them, as we also seek out and appreciate the similarities. It is important to be committed to honoring and caring for the precious divine presence in *their* lives.

Today we are beginning to greatly value the power of Native American spirituality and what we can learn from it.

Cloud of Unknowing

"The universes which are amenable to the intellect can never satisfy the instincts of the heart."

—The Cloud of Unknowing, Anonymous.

I remember flying back to Arkansas from Montana and hoping to see many blue skies above the clouds. The older I get, the more anxious I seem to be on travel days. I wake up in the early morning and look out at Whitefish Lake to see a large cloud just above the water. It seems to be growing and getting closer to the water. There is no sound except for an occasional crow calling nearby, and a slight breeze rustling the aspen leaves in the trees beside the beach. In the morning quiet, the cloud is now turning into fog that is more like a whisper. As it approaches the lake, it gives this spot of northern Montana a mystical countenance.

The 14th-century book, *The Cloud of Unknowing,* by Anonymous, also is a revealing— about Christian mysticism. We call something mystical if it is not obvious to our senses or minds. Something happens when we see such beauty as the clouds and the lake on this cool early morning—something that we cannot explain. It calms my soul on a day when I pray for quietude and patience and flexibility. We acknowledge that our experience tells us *we have known this presence before,* when we took time to be present to it.

That is what I hope was reinforced to me on this trip with my family. I trust I will stay present to the moment and not miss again the many "clouds of unknowing" that are now disappearing, as I have almost finished writing about them. I am going to stop so I can experience them one last time and keep them in my album of preserving the majestic beauty of the precious present.

Nature's Voice

"Happy are those who do not follow the advice of the wicked.
They are like trees planted by streams of water; which yield their fruit in its season, and their leave do not wither."

—Psalm 1:1, 3.

I remember last summer watching the rain come across the lake at Whitefish. As it reaches our shore on a gentle breeze, the small leaves of the willows and aspen trees move back and forth, producing a unique swishing sound. The vibrations caused by the wind and the rain on the fluttering leaves sound like some message they are trying to tell us. Is it a cry for help? Are these the sound of Nature's tears? I don't believe it is a thank you for how we have cared for our natural world.

There is also a fragrance that comes with the sound of rain. It has been called *earthy*. It is thought to be the effect of the earth being moved by the rain. Is it the natural perfume of the earth, calling and enticing us to come and get to know it better in order to care for it?

Almost every person I talk to affirms his or her feeling of God's presence when sitting outside in the natural world. The trees, the sun, the moon, the rain, the flowers, the animals, the mountains, the sea, the earth are healers. They are mood changers. It is difficult not to be grateful, looking across a peaceful lake in the cool mountain air and watching a mother duck gather and care for her eighteen ducklings as the rain has stopped. She makes a distinctive sound as well, maybe telling her ducklings that there is still danger as long as *we* are around.

We are called to care for our churches and places of worship where we experience God. We are called to care for our friends who teach us about the love of God. We are likewise called to care for the natural world, which also calls us back to the Creator God.

God Hole

"There is a really deep well inside me. And in it dwells God. Sometimes I am there too. But more often stones and grit block the well, and God is buried beneath."

—Etty Hillesum in *An Interrupted Life: The Diaries, 1942-1943* and *Letters from Westerbork* (Picador, 1996).

Etty Hillesum was a young Jewish woman studying law in the Netherlands in the 1940s, who lived down the street from Anne Frank. She died at the age of twenty-nine in the Nazi concentration camp at Auschwitz. She kept a diary that described her inner life as well as the severe persecution of the Jews in Holland during those days. It was published after her death. Her transformation from fear and hate to love and care and kindness and compassion for those suffering around her makes her an icon, especially for us today. Through the help of her psychotherapist, she learned to see the "God hole" in people and situations during those amazingly difficult times. And she sought to fill that God hole with the love she had within.

This is indeed our ministry as spiritual friends. Each of us has a hole in our mind, our heart, our body that only God can fill. Instead, we try to fill it with relationships, food, alcohol, drugs, shopping work, sports, work, power—even family, writing, reading, and patriotism. We can also choose to fill it with hate, persecution, bigotry, self-centeredness, intimidation, cruelty, negativity, pessimism, hopelessness, despair, apathy, and indifference.

As spiritual friends we are called to help each other find that God hole and fill it with the best unconditional love we can muster up. It begins with our presence with each other and with holy listening.

I remember a dear friend who came into my office at the hospital early one morning to talk about a relationship that had just ended. He was depressed, sad, broken hearted, in tears. We talked for some time. Mostly I listened and tried to let him know how much I cared about him. Late in the conversation, I mentioned the God hole. Somehow, he intuitively realized that this relationship had completely filled his God hole. I only had to say a few words. A light bulb went on. I usually do not mention the God hole when someone is in so much suffering; but something told me to bring it up on that early morning. Hopefully, both of us were being guided by the Holy Spirit in our own God hole.

Nouwen: Zero-Sum

"'There's not enough love to give to everybody, so I'd better keep my friends for myself to prevent others from taking them away from me.' This is a scarcity mentality. The tragedy is what you cling to ends up rotting in your hands."

—Henri J. M. Nouwen, "Temptation to Hoard" in *Bread for the Journey: A Daybook of Wisdom and Faith* (HarperSanFrancisco, 1997), p. 100.

Nouwen is first describing our life as a zero-sum mentality. In such a world we can do well or win or succeed only if someone else loses; so we are not going to share, because there is only so much food, love, land to go around. There is one pie. If someone takes a slice, it leaves less for the rest of us. One person's gain is another's loss. This theory describes situations in which the total of wins and losses adds up to zero; and thus one party benefits at the direct expense of the other. There is only so much, and not enough for all. Some must lose for others to gain. It is a competitive/scarcity worldview that almost always leads to a fear-based society.

On the other hand, the opposite of the scarcity mentality is a positive-sum situation or abundance mentality, which occurs when the total of gains and losses is greater than zero. A positive-sum plan is possible when resources are seen as abundant and an approach is formulated to satisfy the desires and needs of all concerned. One example would be when two parties both gain financially by participating in a contest, no matter who wins or loses. Positive-sum outcomes occur in instances of distributive bargaining, in which different interests are negotiated so that everyone's needs are met. With an abundancy mentality, there is enough for all.

How we view our neighbors and ourselves and the world is totally different in these two views. A zero-sum life style is isolated and lonely, with our own self-interest guiding us. A positive-sum life sees abundance, gives away food, love, knowledge to those in need; and as Nouwen reminds us, "there are many leftovers."

Jesus' feeding of the five thousand, found in all four Gospels, is a story of a positive-sum experience.

My experience is that I am living in fear—in a zero-sum-life-style mentality—when I am competing with others for the love or attention or support of some entity or person. There is peace in my life when I live knowing there is enough love or support or attention for all.

Dreams

"The Dream will never tell you something you already know."

—Robert Johnson.

I have been in a dream group off and on for many years, and much of our time in spiritual direction training at the Haden Institute at Kanuga was also about dreams. (See: *Unopened Letters from God: Using Biblical Dreams to Unlock Your Nightly Dreams,* by Bob Haden.) In fact, my present spiritual director, Bridget, always asks me as soon as we meet, "Do you have a dream?"

There are some basic principles to understanding dreams, such as the insight that a *house represents you,* and every room is an aspect of you. A car represents your personal energy. However, so much of the symbolism in a dream may be unique to that person.

Three friends once took a dream group for several years to a women's recovery center, where most of the women had a choice of going there or to prison because of alcohol and drug- related abuses. The women had led amazingly hard and grief-stricken lives. These were women who had grown up just like the rest of us, but who had not had the opportunities we had. They were hardened and prematurely aging, but still had a heart of gold. Almost all of their dreams had the same pattern: nightmares, being chased by some awful, violent creatures. Our hearts embraced them. Since we saw them only for a brief time, sometimes the best we could say was that the dream was letting them know that the "dream maker," whom we called God, was letting them know that he or she knew about their terrible situation. There was a

God who cared enough to reveal that *this God knew how much pain they were in and how badly they had been treated.*

Joyce Rockwood Hudson in her book, *Natural Spirituality: A Handbook for Jungian Inner Work in Spiritual Community* (p. 105), believes dreams are the fullest expression of the unconscious. My experience is that dreams are certainly one of many ways God speaks to us, and can be a powerful tool to use in spiritual direction. However, as always, dreams must be approached as we would handle the soul: held gently, honored as bearing a sacred message from one lover to another.

Hillesum: Answers

"{Thinking} may be a fine and noble aid in academic studies, but you can't think your way out of emotional difficulties. That takes something altogether different. You have to make yourself passive then, and just listen. Re-establish contact with a slice of eternity."

—Etty Hillesum in *An Interrupted Life: The Diaries, 1942-1943* and *Letters from Westerbork* (Picador, 1996).

Etty Hillesum gives us her formula for finding her way through difficult situations. Those who make decisions using their thinking (T) function, deciding what is reasonable, will probably disagree. Those who make decisions using their feeling (F) function, taking into consideration the importance of relationships, will likely agree with Hillesum.

Looking deeper, beyond personality types, takes us to another level. I think she is trying to tell us to let the "committee in our head" rest by whatever means we find effective: reading, meditation, music, walking, praying, writing, just being. She is telling us to connect to the God within us however we can. We are to try to find an answer from something greater than ourselves. We do not know the exact answer we will get. We will recognize it, though, because we know it will have something to do with love.

Kayla Mueller: God in Suffering

"I will always seek God. Some people find God in church. Some people find God in nature. Some people find God in love; I find God in suffering. I've known for some time what my life's work is, using my hands as tools to relieve suffering."

—Kayla Mueller (1988–2015) in a letter to her father on his birthday, 2011.

Kayla Mueller was a twenty-six-year-old Christian human rights activist and aid worker from Arizona who was taken captive by ISIS in 2013 in Aleppo, Syria, after leaving a Doctors Without Borders Hospital. Kayla had been involved in the United States with Food Not Bombs; in India with Tibetan refugees; in Israel with African refugees; and in Turkey assisting Syrian refugees. She died in captivity in 2015 after being a hostage for eighteen months and subjected, by all reports, to torture and sexual abuse.

Many have called her "the best of America" and "the best of the millennials." Those who knew her and her suffering in captivity, but themselves escaped, all agree. She certainly should be considered a present-day martyr, as she even tried to relieve the suffering of others who were imprisoned with her. She refused to escape with another young Yazidi girl, telling her, "No, because I am American. If I escape with you, they will do everything to find us again."

God promises to be with us in our suffering. We hear of many who are persecuted who seem to sense God's presence with them; while others talk of being estranged or abandoned by God. Our world so desperately needs more people like Kayla who have the gift of seeing God in the midst of suffering. As we care for and let those who suffer know they are loved, in time, they may again learn to see God in their neighbor. Then, eventually, they may even see God in themselves again. This indeed is our ministry as spiritual friends to each other.

Most of us do not have the overpowering courage and selfless gift of empathy of Kayla; but there are so many ways to let others who are suffering know they are loved. We can sit and listen. We can help with daily tasks that their suffering keeps them from doing. We can visit. We can call. We can volunteer. We can hug. We can read to them. We can feed the hungry. We can be aware of and reach out to and support those who are sick, lonely, poor, weak, homeless. So much more.

Waiting for God

"O Lord, my heart is not lifted up,
My eyes are not raised too high;
I do not occupy myself with things too great and too marvelous for me.
But I have calmed and quieted my soul,
Like a weaned child with its mother;
My soul is like the weaned child that is with me."

—Psalm 131.

I came to early church with all the concerns of the day and the current and past week. I am not playing the harp because I am having difficulty replacing two strings that have recently broken. It was the first meeting for discernment for the Daughters of the King at St. Mark's. We have a wellness forum during the adult formation hour that I have been working on. There are some pages missing in the Altar Book, including the Eucharistic Prayer for the next service. I decide to go and sit at the back of the church to try to quiet my anxiety over these concerns and more. The church is absolutely quiet. The short, simple "green season" hangings are more calming to me, as they are less ornamental than those for other seasons. The candles are lighted and flickering. The spring flowers are displayed in honor of the mother of a friend.

I am in a beautiful place that was built to bring us closer to God; but my head is still a mess. How can I see or taste a fragment of the holy before the service starts? Must I wait for some moment during the liturgy, at the Scripture reading, in the prayers, the sermon, the music, the Eucharist? I pray for guidance, actually for *help*. The message comes. Start intercessory prayers. *You have not said your private prayers this morning before church.* Too busy. I start praying for those I am committed to pray for each day. If I know them, I imagine them with Jesus. Almost immediately, I feel the calm—that peace that passes understanding.

Time after time, this is my experience. I begin to know a peace whenever I can get out of myself and my world and my concerns and send love to my neighbor by visiting, calling, writing, serving, or in a multitude of other ways—but especially through intercessory prayer. I rarely find out how these prayers affect those I pray for; but with each prayer, my mind and my body also take my heart to find Jesus, as I try to connect others to that healing love.

Robert Johnson, Joyce Rockwood Hudson: Dreams Again

"If we try to ignore the inner world, as most of us do, the unconscious will find its way into our lives through pathology: our psychosomatic symptoms, compulsions, depressions, and neuroses."

—Robert Johnson in *Inner Work: Using Dreams and Active Imagination for Personal Growth* (Harper & Row, 1989), p. 11.

My spiritual director best helps me and others connect with God through dreams. Dreams are certainly one way that God, the dream maker, speaks to us. Working with our dreams is like studying a new language. It is the symbolic language of the unconscious. We connect to the unconscious with dreams, imagination, and incidents of synchronicity (or coincidences, or serendipity).

We study our dreams to discover personal symbols that may be specific to us, such as sea and trees for me. There also are collective symbols that may be universal, such as water representing the unconscious; light being our consciousness; a child symbolizing the creative part of us; animals representing instincts; vehicles as our energy, and how we get along with a car expressing our independent energy; buses, planes, trains representing collective energy.

Dreams also speak in the language of mythology, fairytales, religious rituals, music.

Consider learning about dream work as a spiritual practice. Join a dream group, for the gold in dreams can be so much richer when delved for with the help of others. Two books to start with to learn more about dream work are *Inner Work: Using Dreams* and *Active Imagination for Personal Growth,* by Jungian analyst Robert Johnson; and *Natural Spirituality: A Handbook for Jungian Inner Work in Spiritual Community,* by Joyce Rockwood Hudson. Both are also good books to read together in a group.

If this spiritual discipline interests you, just start by keeping an electronic or old-fashioned notebook by your bed, and write down your dreams as soon as you awaken—and see what happens!

De Mello, Ignatius: Consciousness of the Past

"The postulate is that awareness alone will heal, without the need for judgment and resolution. Mere awareness will cause to die whatever is unhealthy and will cause to grow whatever is good and holy."

—Anthony de Mello in *Sadhana: A Way to God* (Image Books).

I try not to read too many de Mello exercises a day in his book, *Sadhana: A Way to God,* but I find myself not being able to wait to read the next installment! As I start to write, I am ending up listing almost all of the exercises as so useful, especially Exercise 30, "Consciousness of the Past," practiced at night. In it we think of our whole day as a film, unwinding the day as though it were a movie, not approving or condemning what we did—just becoming aware.

This is different from the Ignatian Examen, in which we *do* examine and make judgments on our day. In the Examen, we review our day; give thanks; determine where we found God and when we ignored God; recall actions we wish we had not done; ask for forgiveness; and pray for grace for the next day. [See: James Martin, *The Jesuit Guide to (Almost) Everything* (HarperOne, 2010), p. 97.]

De Mello believes, on the other hand, that if only we are aware, *we will heal* without the need for judgment and resolution. The finale of the exercise by de Mello, after we have observed the day as a movie, is noticing *where Christ was with us in the day.* How did Christ act? De Mello asks us to concentrate on how "Christ" acted in our day more than on how *we* acted.

We can find similarities between these spiritual exercises, as well as differences. This is just one more small example of the diversity of methods for becoming aware of our connection to God.

My experience is that when I simply *am aware* and look for Christ through reviewing the movie of my day—God indeed heals—much more slowly than I would like, however. At other times I need the awareness exercises described in the Ignatian Examen to get me back on track.

I am going to have to stop describing all of the de Mello exercises. Otherwise I will be restating his whole book! The miracle of finding and choosing de Mello's book, as well as discovering the exercises of St. Ignatius, was an answer to prayer—and I now share it with you!

Reading Again

"In a course on contemplative prayer, I assigned just six books—and we read them each twice."

—Stephanie Paulsell, "Faith Matters: Reread It Again; The Inexhaustible Spiritual Practice of Rereading," in *The Christian Century* (January 17, 2018), p. 27.

There are so many books I want to read. When friends tell me they are rereading a book, I roll my eyes away from them and wonder about all the other books they are missing. Stephanie Paulsell, a professor at Harvard Divinity School, tells me to roll my eyes back toward my friends and listen to what they are learning.

Certainly, we all have experienced studying again the most reread book, the Bible—especially if we try to follow a systematic study of yearly lectionary readings. It never fails that we see things the second or third or tenth time that we never saw or heard previously—probably because our life experience has deepened and our concentration level has shifted.

How could we have missed before that word or that meaning, or what that person was doing?

During this year I have been blogging about spiritual direction and reconnecting to significant authors and books I have read in the past. I am rereading material I underlined a year ago or ten years ago—and sometimes fifty years ago. As Paulsell suggests, I have become more intimate with the texts and am called to practice more intently some of the teachings presented. I am "continuing to see things I have not seen before. The authors and their books for some reason now more deeply intersect with my life." I must admit that yes, rereading and reconnecting to writers is remembering truths I have forgotten—and seeing truth that I previously overlooked.

Is there any comparison to Bill Murray's experience in the all-time classic movie, *Ground Hog Day?*

Enneagram Retreat and Epiphany

"The good news is we have a God who remembers who we are, the person he knit together in our mother's womb, and he wants to help restore us to our authentic selves."

—Ian Morgan Cron and Suzanne Stabile in *The Road Back to You* (IVP Books, 2016), p. 23.

This past year our rector at St. Mark's, Danny Schieffler, invited the staff to the retreat center for our diocese, Camp Mitchell, to study the enneagram with Presbyterian minister and therapist Rebecca Spooner. Usually staff day-retreats are about planning sessions for the year or exercises using the Myers-Briggs Personality Inventory to help us see how we can relate to each other.

Knowing someone else's enneagram number can be helpful; but the real heart of the enneagram is about personal growth—how to identify the mask *you* have developed for survival. It is designed to enable you to free your true self, the person that God created you to be.

So our rector was giving us a day for our own personal enrichment, away from our usual work, during a busy liturgical season. I wish I had done that for my staff when I was working in the medical field, to let them know how much I cared about their own personal growth. Let this remain an example for all of us.

This was my third enneagram study course. The well-known sin of my enneagram number is pride, and dealing with it was front and center when I heard about the retreat. I already knew all this. Today I am still amazed how things came together at our retreat, and how much more I learned. This is my second lesson. Exposure to a spiritual tool such as the enneagram can be more enlightening each time we go through this process.

We spent a great deal of time on the enneagram during my own preparation to do spiritual direction. More and more I see why. This is a tool to help us know who we really are, the mask we have developed that has become our persona—what everyone else thinks we are, so that we can make our way in the world. Rebecca reminded us of Richard Rohr's famous definition of the enneagram: "the coat and hat we put on to weather the storm."

Assuming this persona has helped us to survive; but now we are searching for our true self, the person God created us to be. Learning about our enneagram number can lead us in the direction of finding our relationship with God that has been blocked for too long by this mask.

The enneagram is not for everyone. Rebecca reminded us that it is only one tool in our spiritual toolbox: If it is helpful, stick with it. If it is not, there are so many other tools to help us connect to God. But if we do relate to it, there is more gold there than we can ever imagine.

This is an ancient tool that has been proven to be true over many centuries. Advent, Epiphany, and Lent are great seasons to spend time expecting more epiphanies about ourselves through the enneagram, especially if we study it with other spiritual friends.

Finding What Is Missing

"What is truth? You can see where there is truth and where there isn't, but I seem to have lost my sight. I see nothing. You boldly settle all the important questions, but tell me, my dear boy, isn't it because you are young and the questions of the world haven't hurt you yet?"

—Anton Chekhov in *The Cherry Orchard*. Premiered 1904.

A dear friend, Pan, who reads my blog, Daily Something, noticed a word I had not spelled correctly. I had been writing about how we see the world through different lenses and glasses. She kindly sent me a message asking: "Did you mean to spell glases with only one s or did you do it to make a point to see if we might see it?" I loved her comment. She reminded me of so many lessons.

It helped me see and remember how something that looks so right can be so wrong. In writing, it more often is a missing letter, especially when there is another similar letter beside it. I have also talked about this phenomenon in my life as a radiologist. Sometimes it was the things that were missing, such as the absence of a part of a bone, that should have clued me in. It was easier to see the things that were added, such as a tumor or extra blood vessels.

So many lessons. We need community to help us have better vision in our world and in our everyday and spiritual lives. I made many fewer mistakes in radiology when I took the time to share with others what I was looking at and asked their opinion. In radiology, that person was a partner or colleague. In writing we might employ a copy editor.

In learning to live life on life's terms, we might consult a therapist. In recovery we would call that person a sponsor. When we want to find out what might be missing in our spiritual life, we can call upon the assistance of a spiritual friend or director.

Gerald May: Dark Night

"Maybe, sometimes, in the midst of things going terribly wrong, something is going just right."

—Gerald G. May, M. D., in *The Dark Night of the Soul: A Psychiatrist Explores the Connection Between Darkness and Spiritual Growth* (HarperOne, 2005).

Gerald May profoundly distinguishes between clinical depression and the dark night of the soul in this book and in *Care of Mind, Care of Spirit*. He speaks to the need to recommend immediate help for those in clinical depression, but sees the dark night as a normal part of the spiritual journey. It is a condition to be "seen through rather than worked through," a cloud of unknowing which often includes a subtraction of prior "knowings" rather than additional knowledge.

The dark night is usually not associated with loss of effectiveness in life or work. One's sense of humor is generally retained. Compassion for others is enhanced after the dark night experience. There is a sense of rightness about it all. Those experiencing it are not pleading for help. The spiritual director and friends of the one in the dark night generally are not frustrated, resentful, or annoyed. May describes clinical depression as the opposite of this condition. May's book on spiritual direction includes extensive examples of good spiritual direction, as well as reminders of pitfalls and how easily we can get off track.

When I pick up his book, I am reminded to approach this ministry of being a spiritual friend with "fear and trembling." Over and over,

May teaches us that we will be good spiritual directors and friends only as long as we stay connected to a spiritual path ourselves and realize that we are simply a vessel.

May: Religion We Choose

"Most of us, having struggled to forge our own autonomous ways in the spiritual life, wind up in some tradition that is not unlike that of our own genetic and cultural forebears."

—Gerald May in *Will and Spirit* (HarperOne, 1982), p. 320.

In *Will and Spirit,* Gerald May writes that at some point it is necessary for us to establish a relationship to some valid existing spiritual tradition. The choices are enormous. We could choose Anglican formality, Roman authority, Quaker simplicity, Methodist fellowship, Presbyterian morality, Baptist freedom, or Evangelical and Pentecostal zeal. We could find ourselves in the center of the Sufi's twirl, in the Navaho's dance, or responding with the correct answer to every Zen koan. All traditions have a core of truth pointing to a single, loving energetic Source of creation.

Polytheistic religions tend to maintain a balance between male and female images of deities; while monotheism fosters a male, father-like image of God. May writes that it is primarily the father's personality that determines the offspring's image of God, even though people learn most of their loving from mothers. May believes that even though the mother plays an important part in our psychological development, fathers are crucial. The monotheistic, male father-like image may become more balanced through devotion to Mary in Roman Catholic Christianity and Eastern Orthodoxy. Rohr and other contemplatives also believe this sole masculine image of God is changed as we relate to the parts of the Trinity as both masculine and feminine.

May: Contemplative Prayer

"There is considerable evidence that highly experienced contemplatives may not have more unitive experiences, but they at least recognize these experiences more often."

—Gerald G. May in *Will and Spirit* (HarperOne, 1982), p. 205.

Gerald May, a psychiatrist associated with the spiritual direction program at the Shalem Institute in Washington, D. C., in *Will and Spirit*, writes about the dynamics of the human mind and its relationship to God in contemplative prayer. May's central theme is the "unitive" experience as the keystone to contemplative spirituality: being at one, loss of self-definition, becoming totally wide awake and open, aware, and compassionate toward others.

This is not something that can be achieved or made to happen. It is a gift from God, given through grace—what those in 12-step programs would call "a moment of clarity" in which the addict or alcoholic briefly glimpses how he or she is relating to the world.

As opposed to a psychedelic experience, which leaves a person right where he or she began, a unitive experience promotes growth or integration. We may put ourselves in position in spiritual direction in order to have such experiences; but it is impossible to *make* them happen. May compares the struggle to that of the addict attempting to quit through willpower over desire. When willpower is all we have, desire wins hands down. The act of legitimate spiritual surrender must be conscious, intentional, and freely chosen, and we must be willing to accept responsibility for surrender.

Contemplative practices may be associated with a greater recognition of the divine in daily life, but they should not to be associated with achievement, attainment, or even a constant state of unity. Emotions must be noted, but left alone. Some contemplatives, such as those who live with chronic pain, and very young children, can be better at this as they tend to stay aware and "keep their hands off their minds."

Pascal asserts that "all human evil comes from our being unable to sit still in a room." The practice of quiet is an exercise in "not doing," a study in surrender, in letting go—which Jung points out is quite different from "doing nothing."

May believes we cannot expect to grow in spiritual awareness without some intentional practice of silence.

Being with the Dying

"When you have sat vigil with a dying soul, you are forever changed. You have experienced a great mystery."

—Megory Anderson in *Attending the Dying: A Handbook of Practical Guidelines* (Morehouse Publishing, 2005).

Megory Anderson has written a large volume on being with the dying, as well as a short pocket-sized handbook on the subject. Many people come for spiritual direction due to to the death of a loved one. Someone significant has died or is about to die. Often the death is very imminent. If there is time, a spiritual director can go over some of the very concrete directions Megory Anderson provides and then gift the person with the small handbook.

My experience is that often there is not enough time for friends even to digest the handbook. Frequently the relative or caregiver is so overwhelmed that even the task of reading is difficult. I had a similar experience with hospice. My father-in-law was put on hospice care the day before he died, and there was so little time for arrangements. We often wait too long before asking for help or accepting the reality of an end-of-life situation.

Anderson teaches us so much. Attending the dying is like the privilege of being at a birthing. It is a sometimes painful celebration of a new life. I especially try to reread Anderson's section about creating a sacred space. It can be helpful to talk to the family about clearing clutter from the room and bringing in sacred objects such as devotional icons, prayer beads, photographs, maybe even childhood books. Helpful activities might include reading beloved stories, even childhood poems; playing favorite music; or lighting a candle. Bringing the person a favorite quilt or fresh flowers from someone's garden could remind everyone that something special is happening here. We come to be with the person who is dying and listen to the person's story. Conversations should be directed to him or her. My experience is always to speak to the dying as if they can hear what we say.

I know of many who, as death approaches, midwife their loved one into a new life by singing favorite hymns, reading the Psalms, taking turns saying prayers, and performing rituals for the dying drawn from their traditions. After the death, saying prayers and preparing the body can be one last loving offering from family and special friends. My father-in-law grew magnificent roses. The night he died, our family took rose petals from the flowers in his room and scattered them over his body before walking his body out to the funeral hearse.

Anderson's book is invaluable to anyone who is attending the dying. The author describes preparation for death, the death process, and what to do afterwards, as well as how to react to unusual behavior from well-meaning family and friends. We so rarely have a guidebook to ease life's more difficult journeys. This is one.

Rohr: Good and God

"God does not love you because you are good; God loves you because God is good."

—Adapted from Richard Rohr, *Things Hidden: Scripture as Spirituality* (Franciscan Media, 2008), pp. 163-164.

We once had a very intelligent friend who told us that as soon as she became a better person, she would come back to the church. I actually hear this same attitude from so many people who come for spiritual direction. They either see church as a house full of hypocrites or as the opposite—a gathering of the most holy among whom they would be deemed unworthy. My favorite answer, of course, is that a church is not a museum for saints, but a hospital for sinners! We go to meet God, to give thanks, to praise God, to ask for forgiveness, and to share the God within each of us with the God in our neighbors. Rohr is teaching us, reminding us that it is God who is the good one—always present, forgiving, supporting, encouraging, loving. This is a hard concept for people who have been raised with a judgmental image of God—because often they as well have unknowingly become most judgmental.

We most often first experience this love by being in community.

Going Upstream

"We are very reasonable creatures, but to feel the grace of God, one must forget about reason and go on a pilgrimage to a place where we no longer 'see as through a glass darkly,' to a place where we are able to see with eyes of gratitude, rather than with eyes of conquest."

—George Grinnell in *Death on the Barrens: A True Story of Courage and Tragedy in the Canadian Arctic* (North Atlantic Books, 2010).

I love to sit by the Mississippi River near Memphis watching barges move slowly upstream, especially on cold, late-January windy mornings. The few dog walkers and runners along the shore move faster than the endless barges churning up white water as they move against the current. The covered barges ride high on the water. They must be empty, but are still straining to travel upstream to be filled somewhere inland on the banks of this mighty river. Where is their destination? St. Louis?

I hope to keep remembering these upstream barges. I like leading my life more easily, moving downstream, going with the flow. Sometimes, however, I am called to go against the crowd, to work my way upstream. It will help if I travel lightly, do not take myself too seriously, do not carry a lot of my own baggage, and do not set out on a right-or-wrong conquest. I know that the journey upstream moves slower than the one downstream; and so I need to remember to speak my truth with gratitude for the opportunity I have been given.

Non-anxious Presence/Or Less Anxious Presence

"The sea does not reward those who are too anxious, too greedy, or too impatient. One should lie empty, open, choiceless as a beach—waiting for a gift from the sea."

—Anne Morrow Lindbergh in *Gift from the Sea* (Pantheon Books, 1955).

Story: Our famous Jane from old school *Dick and Jane* loves her outreach ministry at her church; but sometimes there is chaos and sometimes people get upset at others and are "not Christian." Maybe she should take a geographic cure and go to a more "Christian" church where people get along better.

Response: Former Bishop Maze teaches that if we do not engage in a ministry, we will not stay connected to our church. We discover the ministry God calls us to by learning about our gifts and then offering them to the ministry where the gifts seem to best fit. We follow the most quoted Buechner line about ministry. "The place God calls you to is the place where your deep gladness and the world's deep hunger meet."

Then what happens?

We are humans. Church and all its ministries and groups are part of an organization that is "a hospital for sinners, not a museum for saints." Eventually we are going to run into people problems and relationship difficulties, just as we do at home and work!

Anne Morrow Lindbergh describes our ideal state—the way we would like to be in all our relationships: waiting as "choiceless" as the beach while it anticipates gifts from the sea.

Family Systems dynamics teach us, in the midst of any conflict in a relationship with others, to maintain a state of having the least anxiety—to be a non-anxious presence. If we do this we will make our best contribution toward preventing any tensions from escalating, and eventually will help solve the difficulty. I know of few who can remain non-anxious, for it is not a common human trait. Staying less anxious, however, is a real possibility. If we can be the least anxious presence in any situation, it will keep the arteries in our body from tightening up (a condition that steals minutes, or even weeks from our lifespan). Our inner and outer presence will stay calmer, and we can become a vessel for the Spirit to enter the relationship or situation or meeting or encounter or ministry.

Answer: So how do we become like the beach waiting for the gift from the sea, as Lindbergh is describing? Easy? It involves spiritual disciplines. Prayer and meditation before, during, and after each ministry event is a huge beginning. I am still in the process of learning from others' spiritual disciplines: Centering Prayer, Morning Prayer, yoga, following a rule of life, spiritual direction, worshiping together, studying. There are many more. Our three-legged stool, consisting of tradition, Scripture, and reason, informs us that these disciplines can be gifts from God to help us care for our souls and those of others.

Temple: Church

"The Church is the only society that exists for the benefit of those who are not its members."

—Archbishop William Temple.

Perhaps we should write Archbishop Temple's truth in stone in a prominent place in our churches. It should also be written on our hearts. I also see this declaration as a mission statement for our soul. Jesus gives, in his last discourse to the disciples before he dies, this Great Commandment: "that you love one another as I have loved you" (John 15:12). We are called to stay connected to God's love, and then to share that love with all we meet on this journey. Part of spiritual direction involves helping our spiritual friends stay aware of their connection to God by following a rule of life or observing spiritual practices on a regular basis.

There is a second part to spiritual direction, however. If we just keep that God connection to ourselves and do not pass on the love we have received from God, the love cannot survive.

My image of feeling God's love is like the peace and calm and joy one feels when immersed in the warm water of a bath. We cannot just stay there, however. Our skin shrivels; the water becomes cold and murky and eventually dirty. We are called to enjoy the bath, but then to get out of the bathtub, put some clothes on, and go offer to others what we have to give in words and actions! We may even run a bath for or be called to bathe another. Perhaps we will stoop to wash the feet of others and they will wash ours.

Loving others involves servant ministry. First we must be connected to that love, and then we are to serve through sharing that love with others.

Betsy Singleton: Living in Community at Home

"You never get it all done."

—Betsy Singleton Snyder in *Stepping on Cheerios: Finding God in the Chaos and Clutter of Life* (Abingdon Press, 2017).

Snyder, a Methodist minister and mother of four boys (including triplets)—who was at the time the wife of a member of Congress—wrote in her book about what it is like to stay connected to God in the midst of daily chaos. Some of Snyder's best suggestions for families in *Stepping on Cheerios* are to "take sorta kinda breaks," "have family movie night as a spiritual practice," "be just yourself and nothing else," "nurture something with your kids," "do less comparing," and "stop more." "God made bossy moms" and "everyone screws up" are two other examples of her wisdom that resonated with me.

One of the parts of Snyder's book I treasured is having what she calls "the Squad." This is an extensive list and description of people who helped her out, especially after she had a serious medical complication in her pregnancy. They also came through when her husband, Victor, was in Washington or meeting with his constituents at home.

Snyder and her family are a beautiful example of what living in community is like. Not all of us will have triplets, but all will at some time need the support and love of a community such as Snyder found. It makes all the difference when we are able to receive help—until we can again help others. We become more open to seeing the love of

Christ in our neighbor who reaches out to us. We, in turn, learn from our neighbor more about the Christ in ourselves who guides us to that sacred place of gratitude.

This is a major theme of Snyder's book. She sees lessons in a multitude of situations presented to her, and always moves out of them with gratitude. Gratitude for those who help her, gratitude for lessons she has learned, gratitude for the love of God shown to her family by so many. Her last chapter is titled, "My Cup Runneth Over," as she thanks so many for making her dreams come true.

Rohr: Service

"If your spiritual practice doesn't lead you to some acts of concrete caring or service, then you have every reason not to trust it."

—Richard Rohr, adapted from *Near Occasions of Grace* (Orbis Books, 1993), pp. 107-108.

Richard Rohr gives us an outstanding benchmark to determine if our spiritual practices are relevant—whether a practice is really working for us. If the practice leads to service or caring for others, then we are on the right track. When friends come for spiritual direction and talk about being "dry," this can be a good test to determine if they should change their spiritual practices. If they are still feeling compassion for others, we might suggest that they keep on with the practice a little longer. If there is no concern for others, this may be a sign to try another spiritual practice to reestablish connection to God.

If the Spirit is working in our lives, there is only one way it can go, and that is outward. The Holy Spirit is not a halo; it is more like a river on the move. It can be like the current in the mighty Mississippi flowing downstream to the Gulf of Mexico, sometimes slowly, sometimes rapidly. On occasion, it can be like the rapids on the Snake River. Watch out! We will need to keep our life jackets on and stay close to our community for this one.

When we are connected to the love of God, it must flow outward. When we are aware of God, the Christ within ourselves, it can only branch out and lead us to seeing the Christ in another.

Merton: Epiphany in the World

"In Louisville, at the corner of Fourth and Walnut, in the center of the shopping district, I was suddenly overwhelmed with the realization that I loved all those people, that they were mine and I theirs, that we could not be alien to one another even though we were total strangers."

—Thomas Merton.

This is the first line of Thomas Merton's famous mystical revelation and epiphany which occurred in downtown Louisville, Kentucky. It is described in his journal *Conjectures of a Guilty Bystander* (1968, pp. 140-142).

Merton had been a Trappist monk for seventeen years, and was on an errand for the monastery in the middle of an ordinary day on March 18, 1958. The story became so famous that the city of Louisville erected a plaque at the site in 2008 on the fiftieth anniversary of Merton's revelation. Ordinary people and popes continue to visit the corner of Fourth and Walnut, a site that was life changing for Merton and for those who read his works.

Merton's experience seems similar to what James Finley describes in *Christian Meditation: Experiencing the Presence of God* as "having a finger in the pulse of Christ, realizing oneness with God in life itself."

Merton's epiphany may also be comparable to what St. Francis realized in nature when he called the sun his brother and the moon his sister. Richard Rohr calls it finding our True Self, "our basic and unchangeable identity in God." [1]

Methodists might relate it to John Wesley's experience at 8:45 p. m. on May 24, 1738, at a Society meeting in Aldersgate Street, when someone read from Luther's *Preface to the Epistle to Romans* and Wesley responded: "I felt my heart strangely warmed."[2]

[1]Richard Rohr meditation, Center for Action and Contemplation, "Thomas Merton Part II," October 6, 2017.

[2]John Wesley, *Journal of John Wesley* (London: Charles H. Kelly, 1903), p. 51.

Nouwen: Death

"When we lose a dear friend, someone we have loved deeply, we are left with a grief that can paralyze us emotionally for a long time. People we love become part of us. But as we let go of them they become part of our 'members,' and as we 're-member' them, they become our guides on our spiritual journey."

—Henri Nouwen in *Bread for the Journey* (HarperOne, 2006).

The God of my understanding does not give us a person we love deeply and then let that relationship end with the death of that person. Ours is a God of love. The love from that companion we so deeply cared about is still there with us. We are still in relationship with that person, but in a way we do not understand. Our mutual love does not end. Death is not a period at the end of a sentence, but more like a comma.

Sometimes when we bring to memory events—ordinary as well as special times—with the person we loved, we will also feel that person's presence and wisdom. We can still talk to her or him in this new relationship that is still a mystery. Nouwen believes that sometimes we can be even more intimate in this relationship than we were in life. Love is what continues and never dies.

Some people find it helpful to wear a piece of jewelry or clothing as a physical reminder of a relationship that is now spiritual. Our loved ones are now in some way always present with us, whereas in life they were present only when they were physically with us.

The grief recovery work that we have been involved with for at least twenty years, Walking the Mourner's Path, advocates staying in relationship with our loved one by doing something to honor the relationship we had. When this is followed, amazing transformations have occurred. People have initiated suicide prevention programs, built walking trails, written books, developed new careers in helping professions, built halfway houses for those in recovery, and given land to Habitat for Humanity to honor where their loved one died.

In my case, I returned to church and stopped smoking to honor the life and death of my Grandfather Whaley. My grandfather's love cared for me while he lived and he saved my life even in death. I still feel his presence today, almost forty years later, and especially as I write about him this morning—and now send that love on to my own grandchildren.

Balbir Mathur: Part of the Symphony

"I am one part of the symphony. I know there is an overall scheme to this symphony that I cannot understand. In some way, we are each playing our own part. It is not for me to judge or criticize the life or work of another. All I know is that this is my dance."

—Balbir Mathur in a *Heron Dance* interview (Issue 11) from Inward Outward, Daily Word, October 19, 2016. inwardoutward.org

Our tickets to the Arkansas Symphony are on the third row. At times we do indeed feel as if we are part of the orchestra. We have gotten to know who sits where, when someone new is in a seat, or when a regular is missing. We know a few of the musicians by name. There are still many members of the orchestra playing who were there when we first came to Little Rock more than forty years ago.

I especially remember one moment many years ago when the first cellist had a twenty- second solo very close to the end of the performance. Suddenly his deep, melodious sound was heard above the rest of the orchestra, and then, just as suddenly, he faded back into the background to support the other instruments. I knew that if I had been him, I would have been too nervous the whole night, waiting for that brief time to be the soloist voice soaring above the rest of the orchestra. The professional cellist, of course, seemed as comfortable blended into the orchestra as he was performing his solo. He also continued his direct eye contact with the conductor as he played his brief solo contribution. I later wondered about the many hours he must have practiced in order to perform this part, until the score became almost a part of his being.

The cellist taught me that most of our life is spent being a member of the orchestra with our unique instrument and talents, blending in and brining depth to the composition assigned to us. There will be times when we are called to speak out above the music of the symphony. Before we do this, however, we should be prepared by practicing, knowing intimately our part, especially the timing, and keeping our eye on the conductor. Most of the time, we are called to spend our gifts blending, supporting, and in many ways encouraging the sounds of others.

Lewis: The Great Divorce

"There are only two kinds of people in the end: those who say to God, 'Thy will be done,' and those to whom God says, in the end, 'Thy will be done.'"

—C. S. Lewis in *The Great Divorce* (Geoffrey Bles, 1945).

The Great Divorce is Lewis' classic take on the difference between dwelling in heaven and living in hell. In hell, people become more and more isolated and separated from each other until all communication is lost. Before the great distances develop, there is a bus stop where groups of people in hell are given the opportunity to go to heaven on a tour bus ride, to decide if they might like to live there instead. Spoiler alert! Only one person decides to stay in heaven. The rest return to their life in hell. It is a choice.

With each character that appears, Lewis describes what keeps them in hell. My favorite is the bishop whose intellect dictates that must go back to hell because he is scheduled to give a lecture that he does not want to miss. Some characters remain in hell because they cannot recognize joy; others see all the difficulties in life as someone else's fault; some stay connected to their material goods since they mean the most to them; others find people "beneath them" in heaven. One sees heaven as a trick; and an artist must return to hell to preserve his reputation.

The Great Divorce is a wonderful choice for a book study group, especially in Lent, which will soon be upon us. It can be insightful for people to share with each other which of the characters they most identify with. Lewis hands us a mirror to show us that we do not recognize that we are making choices that result in a hell—ways we have forsaken the gifts of heaven on this earth.

Charleston, Nouwen: Tools, Movements

"What are the tools you use most in building your spiritual life? ... Tools like curiosity and compassion. Like honesty and open-mindedness. There are basic tools like listening and study. There are specialized tools like discernment and meditation. Learning to use the tools from a mentor makes sense and practice is a given. Take care of your tools and they will take care of you: simple spiritual advice."

—Bishop Steven Charleston, Daily Facebook Page.

In his book, *Reaching Out: The Three Movements of the Spiritual Life,* Henri Nouwen describes the spiritual life as "a constant movement between the poles of loneliness and solitude, hostility and hospitality, illusion and prayer." The first movement, from loneliness to solitude, relates to our own spiritual quest to learn more deeply about ourselves. The second movement, from hostility to hospitality, is our spiritual journey leading us to relate to and connect to others. The third movement, from illusion to prayer, is our effort to develop our relationship with God.

Bishop Charleston provides us with tools we can use in every part of all three movements of this journey. Our job as spiritual directors and spiritual friends is to be mentors to each other, employing the contents of our toolbox, sharing our guidebooks of how we have used these tools, and sharing our tattered and frayed maps of which road to take down each of these movements or paths. This cooperation also entails filling in for each other or becoming a place of respite when one of us runs out of gas. We might also take turns providing a picnic of spiritual food as we travel together in community.

Silence, Waiting for Dolphins, Chant

"When chant music stops, sometimes quite abruptly, an audible silence reverberates throughout the room, especially in the high arches of the oratories in which it is sung. If we listen carefully, we discover that … chant inducts us into this silence that is the ground of our being."

—David Steindl-Rast, O.S.B., in *The Music of Silence: Entering the Sacred Rhythms of Monastic Experience* (HarperCollins, 1995).

We have often sat silently on a balcony overlooking the Gulf in the early morning, watching, anticipating the sunrise, waiting for the dolphins to make their first run. Then we wait for a line of pelicans to silently sweep by. The rhythm of the waves is like a heartbeat. Today it is a slowly beating heart. Yesterday the heartbeat was faster.

At home in Arkansas, we sit with our son and his family on his back deck as the sun sets behind the woods and wait for the hummingbirds to come and feed before they finally rest for the evening. Nature seems to be calling us to be still, to wait. Our own heartbeat slows. Our bodies seem to confirm that we are connecting to something greater than ourselves. Our minds want to repeat Julian of Norwich's famous words, "… and all shall be well, and all shall be well, and all manner of things shall be well." We are ready for whatever comes. We think. *Maybe.* The dryer stops working. We know whom to call for help, and again we wait—now for the repair workers to come. We pray to take time between tasks, between breakdowns.

What do we do between sunrise, dolphins, pelican, sunset, and hummingbird times? One more suggestion is: wait for the heartbeat of music, especially the "silence between the notes" of Gregorian Chant. One of the most popular versions to listen to has been *CHANT* by the Benedictine monks of Santo Domingo de Silos. If you get "hooked," you may want to read their companion book, *The Music of Silence,* by Brother David Steindl-Rast, O.S.B., which may then lead you to a desire to follow in some form the Canonical Hours or seasons of the day. Another related book is simply called, *CHANT,* by Katharine Le Mee, who tells you more about the origins, form, practice, and healing power of Gregorian Chant.

God is constantly calling to us; but God seems for many to speak most clearly in the silence between sunrise, pelican, dolphin, chant, and sunset hummingbird times.

Taylor: Spiritual Direction in the World

"People can learn as much about the ways of God from business deals gone bad or sparrows falling to the ground as they can from reciting the books of the Bible in order."

—Barbara Brown Taylor in *An Altar in the World* (HarperOne, 2009).

I received this quote from Barbara Brown Taylor today from *Synthesis: A Weekly Resource for Preaching and Worship in the Episcopal Tradition* (synthesispub.com). I look to my right, at the new bookcase my husband bought me, containing all the books that I want to share with you this year about spiritual direction. Then I look straight ahead out of a floor-to- ceiling window and watch a gentle spring rain bathe the trees between our house and our neighbors'. I can hear the rhythm of the rain on the roof above, where there is very little insulation in our "modern" 1960s home.

We will soon have dinner with our children and grandchildren in their new home across the street. What a blessing just to walk across the road to be with grandchildren, our greatest gifts, our most important visitors we will entertain. I learn from them every time about simple joy and unconditional love and wide-eyed excitement for life. I hope I can hold on to my gratitude for them that I have learned from Barbara Brown Taylor. She was a speaker recently at the Buechner Writing For Your Life Conference in Nashville I attended at Belmont University. She is still the amazing writer, speaker, and teacher she was when I first read her books more than thirty years ago. If you have a chance to hear her, don't miss it.

She has taught all of us how to continue to be aware of the "altars" in the world that keep us constantly connected to the God of our understanding. We will see them too, if only we have eyes and ears and hearts and hands—and even noses to smell. Yes, the smell of a spring rain is not unlike the fragrance of the well-known costly incense used at Smoky Mary's in Manhattan (Church of St. Mary the Virgin). The altars in our churches are also thin places where we go regularly to give thanks for the "other" altars out in the world.

Addiction and Spiritual Direction

"We have entered into the world of the Spirit. Our next function is to grow in understanding and effectiveness. This is not an overnight matter. It should continue for our lifetime."

—*The Big Book of Alcoholics Anonymous,* 4th edition (Alcoholics Anonymous World Services, 2001), p. 84.

Sometimes those coming to me for spiritual direction are blocked because of addiction. They have filled their "God hole" with another form of spirit, alcohol or drugs, and this is no longer working. How do we help spiritual friends who need recovery? First of all, as you know, this is a disease, not a moral failing. And denial is a HUGE part of the disease. It is the only disease that tells you that *you do not have the disease;* so look for subtle hints. If this comes up, it could be a time to suggest the name of a therapist specializing in addiction, or a good friend of theirs who is in a recovery program. People in recovery will simply tell a listener their story— what it was like when they were drinking, and now what their life is like in a recovery or 12-step program. This should become a two-way street. Telling their story keeps them sober as well as possibly helping someone else. I know of no more powerful act of love than being vulnerable enough to tell someone else your story about how another, a new Spirit, has entered your life and made all the difference.

Most people have no idea how spiritual 12-step programs are. They offer a new way of life, a road less traveled. Statistics say that only about ten percent of people with alcohol addiction make it to recovery. Recovery is not just about not drinking; it provides an entirely new perspective: looking at and relating to the world with a new pair of glasses. Alcohol might have been a way to cope with living life on life's terms. After we stop drinking we will need a new coping method, which is a relationship with a higher power that most call God.

I remember, when I first started going to a 12-step program, that I soon believed it would be impossible for me to recover, when I was told that the heart of this program was spiritual. I already was a very spiritual person, leading groups, writing articles about faith! However, I soon realized that God was a *part* of my life, but *I* was in charge—the pilot; and I gave God the position of co-pilot, being there to help me with my plans. I had been told this in church, of course, since an early age: to put *God* in charge of my life. But I had to hear it someplace else to develop the incentive to change—for, you see, I have such good ideas!

Charleston: Watched Over

"They are watching over you, the ones who have gone before, the ones who know you best, the spirits of a love that never dies, your ancestors of hope and courage, those bright souls who shaped your life and gave you life and showed you what life really was."

—Bishop Steven Charleston, Daily Facebook Page.

I know I am watched over by loved ones who have died. I have no doubt about it. There are times when I am able to do things I *know* I could never do alone, without being helped and cared for by others. My grandfather was the most important person in my growing up years; he taught me about unconditional love. When he died, I was devastated. I wanted to do something to honor him. I knew he did not like my smoking. I had tried to quit many times without success. Quitting smoking for me was a spiritual experience. I have not had a cigarette since December 7, 1979, the day of my grandfather's funeral. My grandfather loved me when he was living and saved my life after he died.

One New Year's Eve, I walked the labyrinth at Christ Church. It was a cool night and I was wearing a long, black shawl with fringes like ones you sometimes see over pianos. Suddenly, during the walk, I felt the presence of my grandmothers holding me on both sides, like the shawl around my shoulders, or the one that Elijah left for Elisha.

This weekend I had a dream that I received a letter from Peggy Hayes, my former spiritual director. I knew it was from her because of the address and writing; but I woke up before I could read her handwritten message on the short, folded-up letter. My prayers have been asking what was in the letter. I am planning to ask my dream group about it for their input this morning.

Buechner: Meditation

'If you compare the mind to a balloon, meditation as a religious technique is the process of inflating it with a single thought to the point where the balloon finally bursts and there is no longer even the thinnest skin between what is inside it and what is outside it."

—Frederick Buechner in *Wishful Thinking: A Seeker's ABC* (HarperSanFrancisco, 1973).

Buechner so often takes us "out of the box." Certainly, we hope in meditation to enter that thin place where the spiritual and the real word nearly touch. Buechner tells us that meditation can not only dissolve that thin membrane, but break it wide open, so it no longer exists. That definitely is what happens when we see the Christ in our neighbor and our neighbor sees the Christ in us. It certainly happens when we recognize the sacredness in the secular world; when we honor every human being; when we care for "this earth, our island home." That barrier often is broken in the Sacraments, especially the Eucharist and Baptism. We experienced it at our church yesterday at the baptism of three adults; but something happens with infant baptism as well. Earthy holiness breaks through, all wet and sometimes screaming.

I like the image of the bursting balloon, because we never know when it will happen. Balloons, similar to meditation practices, come in all sizes and shapes and colors. Some balloons seem unbreakable. Others burst with little effort. It is a mystery. Breaking a balloon also can produce chaos. And that can be where God most often meets us.

Nouwen: Choosing Life

"The most important question is not 'Do I kill?' but 'Do I carry a blessing in my heart or a curse?' The bullet that kills is only the final instrument of the hatred that began being nurtured in the heart long before the gun was picked up."

—Henri Nouwen in *Bread for the Journey* (HarperSanFrancisco, 1997).

Nouwen reminds us that at the root of most of the warring factions and killings today are events in which *love left a person's heart*. The shooters often no longer feel or perceive love. Sometimes love is present, but due to mental illness, abusers cannot perceive it. Sometimes living in a culture of constant violence takes that love away. Sometimes poverty and what is required to survive may lead sufferers to a loveless life. There are so many scenarios.

Our ministry in the outside world is to bring love to the people we encounter, wherever we are, wherever we go. This may not be easy, but we do not have a choice if we care about the world we leave for our children and grandchildren. How we treat, how we greet people on the street, at the grocery store, at the gas station, at the food pantry could prevent more than one act of violence if we are able to give people a hint that they are loved and valuable.

How do we keep love in our own hearts to share? There are a multitude of ways. We know that love is something that only multiplies when it is given away.

All of the spiritual exercises and disciplines have been developed over centuries by people trying to connect us to the God of love.

How do we keep the God of our understanding as *the God of love* rather than the angry or wrathful God that some have been led to believe in? My experience is that when we stay positive, when we live a life of gratitude, when we keep realizing the gifts we have been given and how we are cared for even in the most difficult times, *love stays with us*. For Christians it is the light of Christ living in our hearts.

It also helps to be around others who are sharing love, those in whom we can so easily see the love, the light of Christ in their hearts. Love is contagious.

Palmer: Acquired Taste

"I believe that Christian Formation, the main task of the church, is the way God teaches our hearts to long for and love things, people, and God in the right way. It is through attending to my Rule of Life—the holy habits of weekly Eucharist, daily prayer, regular acts of service, study, and reflection, that God teaches me to love in the right way. It is kind of like God's way of instilling in us a taste for the Kingdom of God, because the Kingdom of God … is an acquired taste."

—Trent Palmer, a member of St. Paul's Episcopal Church, Fayetteville, Arkansas, on St. Paul's Morning Reflection.

Friend and former Methodist minister, Trent Palmer, makes us look up and take notice when he says "the Kingdom of God is an acquired taste." Those who are connected to some form of a sacramental church where the Eucharist or Communion is central to worship may especially relate to the idea of using our sense of taste to know God.

I think of the many opportunities to taste the Kingdom on the smorgasbord that God provides. Some take a few bits of the Kingdom and decide for many reasons that it is not their cup of tea. There are others who experience only a small taste of the Kingdom of God and its peace and crave more. Sometimes that craving lasts for a lifetime. But at other times the busyness of the world deadens our taste or keeps us from the table. Tasting the Kingdom is so much like the parable of the seeds that fall on the path, in the thorns, on rocky ground, and in good soil.

Tasting the Kingdom can be compared to what a person new to recovery is told. You don't just go to one meeting or meet once with a sponsor and then *you are in recovery*. Rather, you go to ninety meetings in ninety days and you met regularly with a sponsor—and you connect to the program for the rest of your life.

My daughter and I wrote a book, *Taste and See: Experiences of God's Goodness Through Stories, Poems, and Food, As Seen by a Mother and Daughter*. We wrote about our experiences of seeing God's presence in difficult times, and food was always present. God uses all of our senses and more to keep us connected.

I always look to the menu plan that God provides. When we taste the fruit of the Spirit— peace, joy, love, patience, kindness, goodness, faithfulness, gentleness, and self-control—we will know we are living in the Kingdom.

Guenther: At Home in the World

"Inevitably, even if we are persistent and faithful, there will come a time when God seems not to be listening or speaking to us. We have entered a desert time."

—Margaret Guenther in *At Home in the World: A Rule of Life for the Rest of Us* (Seabury Books, 2006).

Well-known author and Episcopal priest Margaret Guenther reminds us that we do not come into the world equipped with a spiritual road map or owner's manual; therefore we need to write our own. We cannot download from some celestial source a spiritual MapQuest with precise directions for turning each corner.

Guenther gives us an easily readable book about how to follow a rule of life and still live in the world. Our rule will be different at varying stages of our lives. She offers ways to live in the awareness of the preciousness of each day, valuing every day as if it were our last, constantly reminding ourselves that time is a gift from God. Each chapter discusses a distinctive aspect of our lives, our families, our solitude, our creativity, our money, our fear of abundance, our friends and enemies, our prayer, and our use of power.

The chapters are followed by questions for reflection, making the book an excellent choice for a small group study.

I keep reading *At Home* and still learn something surprising or consider a new practice whenever I pick up the book. Guenther suggests that whenever a person comes to mind, we should call, visit, send a text, or lift up a prayer. I also learned this from my spiritual director in deacon training, Dan McKee.

Guenther discusses how Sabbath is not merely ceasing to work but a dedication to *celebrating something that makes us new,* something that re-creates ourselves. She reminds us that an ongoing association with children, "who live closer to the ground" than we do, can be a powerful source for our own re-creation.

Guenther consoles me when forgiveness comes too slowly. She describes forgiveness as a great block of ice that melts slowly and cannot be hurried. "There is no spiritual equivalent of a microwave."

Today she reminds us what may be going on when we feel spiritually dry. She suggests we reexamine our spiritual practices. Perhaps the spiritual tools we are using have becomes idols. Our form of prayer becomes more important than prayer. We become so intent on following our rule of life that we forget its purpose..

Buechner: Spiritual Gifts

"The "place God calls you to is the place where your deep gladness and the world's deep hunger meet."

—Frederick Buechner in *Wishful Thinking* (Harper & Row, 1973).

As usual, Frederick Buechner, in perhaps his most quoted phrase, gives us the best advice about how to find our ministry. We are given gifts from the Spirit for our ministry, for the doing of God's work. As with "the varieties of gifts" mentioned in 1 Corinthians 12, there are a variety of "spiritual gifts inventories." I was reminded at a recent presentation by The Rev. Dr. Kate Alexander that we must not limit what we think our spiritual gifts might be to only those gifts described in biblical times. And we also cannot assume that every spiritual gift must seem "spiritual." She gave the example of the very detailed work of proofreading the Sunday bulletin as an important ministry. We are to remember that all the gifts serve to further the work of God, not necessarily *our work* or *our agenda* or *our goals.*

In addition to several inventories, material from the Stephen Ministry by Stephen Haugk leads us through other clues to our spiritual gifts. The gifts we see in our most admired person may also be ours. The gift we use to bring about our most fulfilling life event may be our gift. The actions of Jesus we most admire may be our gift. I also learned from Lloyd Edwards in his book, *Discerning Your Spiritual Gifts,* that significant gifts may come out of our woundedness. For example, those in recovery best stay in recovery by helping others find freedom from addictions. Those who have experienced the death of a significant person are often the ones who can later best help heal others who are grieving.

Parker Palmer's book, *Let Your Life Speak,* is another classic book about where and how God leads us into the servant ministry of using our spiritual gifts.

My experience is that I think I am using my gift when I am energized by the ministry in which I am involved. I put energy in and more comes out. The tried and true biblical fruit of the Spirit can also be an indicator of when we are using our spiritual gifts. Galatians 5 tells us we will feel and know "love, joy, peace, patience, kindness, goodness, faithfulness, gentleness, self-control" when we are connected to or guided by the Spirit.

Nouwen, Merton: Meditative Prayer

"Many voices ask for our attention. 'Be sure to become successful, popular, and powerful.' But underneath all these often very noisy voices is a still, small voice that says, 'You are my Beloved, my favor rests on you.' To hear that voice requires solitude, silence, and a strong determination to listen."

—Henri Nouwen in *Bread for the Journey* (HarperSanFrancisco, 1997).

Nouwen so often calls us to this still small voice that speaks to us in silence and meditative prayer. This also is a calling of Thomas Merton.

I have tried to read Thomas Merton's work in the past, but could not connect with it. So when I spied his very short treatise, *Spiritual Direction and Meditation,* I decided it was time to give him another try, especially when so many contemporary spiritual writers such as Henri Nouwen keep quoting him. Merton's book was published in 1960, and therefore we must forgive his exclusively masculine usage. It is important to remember that he wrote to people with a Catholic religious background, and Catholic clergy in particular, addressing many issues helpful to a young male novice.

The book, however, is filled with pearls in almost every sentence. Merton constantly reminds us that the ultimate end of meditation is communion with God *directly,* in the present—the awakening of our inner, true self and positioning of ourselves toward the Holy Spirit so that we will be able to respond to God's grace. We hope to see the mysteries of the life of Christ as a part of our own spiritual existence.

Merton outlines the simple essentials of meditative prayer:

1. We first must be sincere about praying.

2. We are to attempt to focus on meditating.

3. We sincerely hope for a divine union with God.

4. We then rest contently in God's presence.

The precise way we make our meditation depends on our temperament and natural gifts. For the intellectual, the thinking person, the mind must ascend by reasoning to the threshold of intuition. All thinking processes must end in love.

Those with more feeling and intuitive minds may approach the truth almost immediately, apprehending the wholeness as beauty rather than truth. Those with an intuitive temperament may be able to use all their senses to place themselves into the life of Jesus and connect spiritually to Christ.

The writings of Merton and Nouwen so often lead us to contemplative meditation, spiritual direction, liturgical prayer, and the Eucharist—all of which seek the same end, a deeper union with Christ.

Working Class Spirituality

"I think you have to put a little sweat equity into what you believe. You have to practice what you preach. Justice does not just happen. Compassion is not a spectator sport, but something I have to exercise as I roll up my sleeves to do my part in creating a better community. I need to put in my hours as a volunteer. I have to join the prayer crew and put my life on the line to make a difference. The world will not change by wishes, but by the labor of love we call faith. Spirituality is not a spa but a construction site where we build hope one heart at a time."

—Bishop Steven Charleston, Daily Facebook Page.

Oh, goodness! I love to sit and meditate and walk and write and read and wait in silence and go to weekly Eucharist. Bishop Charleston reminds us that being a Christian is not a spectator sport. Eventually all of our spiritual practices connecting us to God will be calling us to some action, a reaching out of ourselves in some way. Even when we are homebound we can call or write or cook or knit or invite others in.

My experience is that we do not have to go out of our way to realize what we are called to do. Each task will present itself to us daily. A person will come to guide us or suggest something. Someone in need will appear. Suddenly we will see a situation that was always there that calls us to reach out. Often the problem is that we become aware of so many needs around us that we can be overwhelmed. Buechner gives us a good formula for determining our next step. We are called to the place where *the world's deep hunger and our deep gladness meet*. We look for where our passion is, where we are energized to get to work.

We will soon learn that we are not necessarily called to the ministry that our parents or our friends or the world thinks we should do. We are opened up to do work that is *our* passion, work that we would do for no compensation. There we will begin to accomplish things we never thought we were capable of doing, and increase in energy rather than becoming depleted.

When we find this calling, we start becoming the person God created us to be.

Kelsey: Outreach

"A Christian meditative practice that does not result in horizontal outreach to suffering and lost human beings has gone astray."

—Morton Kelsey in *Companions of the Inner Way: The Art of Spiritual Guidance* (Crossroad, 1983), p. 27.

Morton Kelsey was a teacher, counselor, Episcopal priest, former teacher at Notre Dame University, and author of more than thirty books on spiritual development.

He writes about the tension that develops between the peace we find in relationship to God and the unrest that dominates our outer world. This tension is similar to what we heard Gordon Cosby from Church of the Saviour write about recently. Cosby called it the real and unreal world. In fact, the Church of the Saviour's website is titled Inward Outward.

Just as inner peace is brought about through love, the same is true for birthing outer peace. The love we find in staying connected to the God of our understanding calls us out of ourselves to those who are suffering in the world. The paradox is that in reaching out to those in need, we again find God, for that is where God promises to be most present.

Spiritual friends who have encountered the creative love of Christ within themselves and in others can be guides to practices that will put us in position to experience this kind of love. Often spiritual guides are helpful in pointing out to us where God was working in our life, where we experienced God's love and protection, and perhaps were not aware of it. Spiritual friends can lead us to the Christ who is already within us—which then prompts *us* to find the Christ in our neighbor, especially our neighbor in need.

Keller, Tillich, Lamott: Faith, Doubts

"Observers in the full enjoyment of their bodily senses pity me, but it is because they do not see the golden chamber in my life where I dwell delighted; for, dark as my path may seem to them, I carry a magic light in my heart."

—Helen Keller in *Midstream: My Later Life* (Sun Dial Press, 1929).

How beautifully Helen Keller illuminates her faith. Someone who is blind describes faith as light, a light in her heart. She also does not deny the presence of doubt. The words of Paul Tillich which Ann Lamott has popularized ring in my ears, "The opposite of faith is not doubt but certainty." Faith implies believing in something or being in relationship with something that is a mystery, that is not defined by our human understanding.

Our rational minds can take us only so far in understanding faith.

When a person has difficulty with mystery, doubts move in. Our doubts can be stepping- stones to a deeper faith as we read and share our uncertainties with others and learn and experience the mystery together.

I so often speak with spiritual friends about this and reassure them that doubt is not unnatural or unhealthy or the enemy. I tell friends, "Let's talk about your doubts. If you come to a place of unbelief, let me carry your faith until you are ready to take it back. I am counting on you to do the same for me when I am overshadowed by doubt."

Buechner: Surprise Visits

"Jesus is apt to come, into the very midst of life at its most real and inescapable. Not in a blaze of unearthly light, not in the midst of a sermon, not in the throes of some kind of religious daydream, but ... at supper time, or walking along a road."

—Frederick Buechner in *The Magnificent Defeat* (Harper & Row, 1966).

Buechner describes how we see Jesus in our lives, in our real lives. We do not necessarily need to go on some great pilgrimage or be in an ancient cathedral. God is all around us in our tasks and routines. Our ministry as spiritual friends is helping each other see God in our everyday lives.

All of the Bible's resurrection stories give us many clues as to where and how to find Jesus. Jesus's resurrection appearance is a surprise to the disciples on the road to Emmaus, to Mary at the tomb, to the disciples locked in the upper room, to the disciples fishing. It is off of the agenda. Jesus is usually not immediately recognized. Jesus engages in ordinary actions such as cooking and eating and walking. He looks like an ordinary person, but may do extraordinary things such as walking through walls. Jesus still bears his wounds, but they are healed. Jesus feeds us. Jesus calls us by name. Jesus makes himself known to ordinary people. With the exception of Jesus' appearance to Paul on the road to Damascus, Jesus appears to those who know him. Most importantly, Jesus speaks truth and love and peace.

If you want to know more about resurrection, meditate again on these resurrection stories, which we will soon hear again.

Nighttime Prayers, Compline

"Keep watch, dear Lord, with those who work, or watch, or weep this night, and give your angels charge over those who sleep.
Tend the sick, Lord Christ; give rest to the weary, bless the dying, soothe the suffering, pity the afflicted, shield the joyous; and all for your love's sake. Amen."

—St. Augustine of Hippo, *The Book of Common Prayer,* p. 134.

This gift from St. Augustine is one of the nighttime prayers from Compline, an evening service to be read just before bedtime. The brief prayer service can be said by individuals, but also by families or groups who are gathering just before retiring. I particularly remember when our friends Barbara and Hap Hoffman came to our house and said Compline with our family every night for six weeks while I was recovering from surgery.

In my medical practice, this prayer was especially meaningful, as I could visualize the people I knew working at night at our Children's Hospital and the patients we were all helping to care for. This prayer also gave me strength when I was on call at the hospital at night, knowing that there were people all over the globe saying these prayers. As Compline became a more regular part of my rule of life, I began to visualize people in other professions working at night in grocery stores, restaurants, airports, or police stations. I remembered the dying, as well as those mourning the death of a loved one. I began praying for the joyous.

All of these prayers ever so briefly have helped me get out of myself and all my problems, as I began praying for and thinking about others. This service calms my soul, and is better than any sleeping pill or drug or drink.

There are also beautiful nighttime prayers in *A New Zealand Prayer Book* (HarperCollins, 1989). I especially relate to one line, "what has been done has been done; what has not been done, let it be" (p. 184).

I keep remembering the C. S. Lewis quote you will often hear from me, "We do not pray to change God. We pray to change ourselves." We can be especially vulnerable and therefore open to change as we offer our nighttime prayers.

Acknowledgements

Thank you to Beth Lambert, Paula Martin, and Isabel Anders whose guidance, encouragement, and expertise made this book possible.

Made in the USA
Columbia, SC
04 September 2019